YANKEE

DICTIONARY

BY THE SAME AUTHOR:

No Ship May Sail

You Need a Complete Rest

Eastward the Sea

YANKEE DICTIONARY

A Compendium of
Useful and Entertaining Expressions
Indigenous to New England

By

CHARLES F. HAYWOOD

Published By

JACKSON & PHILLIPS, INC.

LYNN, MASSACHUSETTS

YANKEE DICTIONARY

I dedicate this book to my father, Charles Edward Haywood, and my mother, Anne Moulton Haywood, both of whom loved Old New England, its life, its people, its history, its customs and its speech.

ACKNOWLEDGEMENTS

I gratefully acknowledge the assistance, suggestions and counsel of the following, who are of a tradition deeply rooted in Old New England; Roscoe W. Hilliker of Lynn, Alton Hall Blackington of Beverly Farms, Margaret Hallett Wade of Quincy, Thomas G. Howarth of Manchester, Massachusetts, Theodora A. Gerould of Westmoreland, New Hampshire, Mary L. Lamprey of North Easton, Massachusetts, George McBrien of Swampscott, Guy Northey of Lynn, Mildred Halvorson of Salem, Robert Cleaves, Jr. of Cohasset and Daniel J. O'Brien of the Boston Globe.

Especially am I indebted to my wife, Dorothy C. Haywood, Chief Librarian of the Lynn Public Library and her Reference Department staff, who have so expertly made available the unusual resources of their collection.

Some of the definitions in this book have been published previously in *Boston Sunday Globe Magazine, Boston Bar Journal,* and *Dartmouth Alumni Magazine.*

PREFACE

That a dictionary may be entertaining even while imparting knowledge and culture, is, we fully realize, a quite novel concept. Yet this is precisely what we seek to do now with YANKEE DICTIONARY, a newcomer in the lexicographical world. We dare attempt to entertain the seeker after knowledge because we deal with a very interesting fellow, to wit; the New England Yankee.

Noah Webster, Samuel Johnson and their many worthy successors did not undertake to be interesting for the excellent reason that they thought the generality of mankind mistrusts knowledge unless it be tedious. We do not agree; hence the manner and style in which this volume of lexicographical exactitude is written.

YANKEE DICTIONARY differs from its fellow lexicons in that it cannot pretend to be comprehensive and all inclusive. The reason for this is plain. No group of scholars, not even the learned savants who have labored in the creation of this volume, could hope ever to become familiar with all the words, expressions and things peculiar to this region the Yankees call their own.

So we present in YANKEE DICTIONARY what we now have, assuring the reader who vainly searches for something he feels should be here and is not, that our staff of lexicographers continue with their work in the hope of capturing in print much more that is at this time legendary, traditional and apocryphal.　　　　CHARLES F. HAYWOOD

ACCOMMODATION

 The train that made every station on the line, dropping off mail for each village post office, taking aboard the outgoing pouch and unloading from the express car various items, perhaps a crated bath tub, a half dozen cans of paint, a trunk for a summer visitor, a new cutter bar for a mowing machine. The low wheeled little locomotive on the head end, often a Mogul type, had plenty of power to start the train if the station was at the foot of a grade or on a curve. Behind the engine was a mail car loaded with dozens of half full bags for the towns along the line. Then came the express car, stacked with boxes and crates and barrels of merchandise, its doors wide enough so a coffin could conveniently be unloaded, for from time to time a boy who had lived most of his adult life in the big city was shipped home to be laid away with his folks up there under the elms in the graveyard on Green Hill. After the head end cars came a smoker full of drummers, farmers who had been doing some purchasing in town and railroad men dead-heading to work. Tall stories and tobacco smoke abounded in this car. A coach in which the ladies might ride was generally the last car in this little train that went puffing up the valley, taking care of the stations that the limited roared through with throttle wide open.

1

AFOOT OR AHOSSBACK

Another one of the "He don't know" expressions. When a Yankee says "He don't know whether he's afoot or ahossback," he means that the person to whom reference is made is in a bemused and be-puzzled state, to wit; a quandary. Or perhaps he means that the fellow lacks sufficient mental acuity to know where he is going or how. Note carefully that anyone who lets the sound of the letter "R" creep into this expression is no Yankee.

ALEWIFE

One of the herring family, it lives most of its adult life in the sea, returning to fresh water to spawn in April and May. Rapids and waterfalls are no obstacle; they commonly negotiate an almost ver-ticle climb several times their own length. To under-stand their strength and power, one must realize that it is as if a man could leap over his garage roof. The Indians awaited the spring alewife run to enjoy a season of easily caught fresh fish; the early settlers learned quickly, but went the red men one better, used nets and salted the catch down in barrels. Since unregulated man can destroy the sources of his own wealth, the states have enacted statutes to prevent the people from catching the entire spring alewife run, thus making extinct the species. Conservation procedure usually is for the town to auction the privilege to set nets to one person, requiring him to close his traps on alternate days so half the alewives may reach their ultimate destiny in their spawning ground. This operation is regularly inspected by a state conservation officer. Townspeople are allowed to take enough fish for their personal use and they frequently manage enough extra to have one alewife in each hill of corn, a fertilizing technique the early Yankees learned from the Indians. Some towns have constructed a channel with a "Y" in it and the nets may be set in only one branch, thus permitting half the fish to swim safely upstream. Many Yankee towns still have their alewife runs, although here and there an ancient stream has been so obstructed or polluted that the instinct of the fish tells them to avoid the locality.

AN ALEWIFE IN HIS AIR CHAMBER

When the old timers said this of a man, they meant he was not performing at all well and offering some lame excuse to explain a poor job. An expression common only in seacoast towns, it originated the day two handtubs had a contest on a fine spring afternoon when the alewives were running. Both Engine 8 and Engine 9 dropped their suction pipes

3

in Strawberry Brook and went furiously at it to see which could throw the longest stream. The issue was in doubt, the judges were undecided and then No. 9's stream commenced to fail, dwindling to a dribble not strong enough to extinguish a fire in a hen house. English 8 departed in triumph with the prize, leaving 9's men profanely disassembling their handtub to see what ailed their machine. Next day the word around town was that an alewife a foot long had been taken in from the brook through the No. 9's suction pipe and lodged in the pump's air chamber, thus ruining their stream. No. 8 and every other fire company scoffed and made insulting remarks by the dozen. No. 9's men said they would punch anyone in the nose who questioned the veracity of their explanation and a few took them up on this offer. The argument died down after several good fist fights, but the expression remained, and from then on anyone who offered what sounded like a weak excuse was asked if he had an alewife in his air chamber.

ALOFT

Ordinarily the sailor's expression for any thing concerning masts, rigging, spars and sails above the deck. What concerned the ship from deck to keel was 'Alow" and when life was completely satisfactory the windjammer sailor said "All's well alow and aloft." In the old days "aloft" had a second meaning; the Eastern part of the Mediterranean. To understand how the mariners of long ago came to develop this expression, one must first realize that jack tar is usually an imaginative fellow. Then, looking at a chart of the Mediterranean, we will see that it is long and narrow with other bodies of water such as the Adriatic, the Aegean, the Tyrrhenian, the Gulf of Sirte and the Dardanelles at right angles to the main body of the sea. So to the sailor man a 2000 mile voyage east from Gibraltar to Smyrna seemed to him in his imagination like climbing aloft on a very tall mast and if he changed course and sailed north for Marseilles or Trieste or a Greek port he felt that he was going out on the yard arm of a square rigger. Therefore we read in old records that this or that ship was "aloft," meaning she was somewhere east of "The Rock" trading here and there in Italy or Crete or Egypt or France for cargo and expected, some fine day, to show her topsails in the outer reaches of Gibraltar harbor, call for mail, wood and water and then head west across the stormy Atlantic, homeward bound at last.

ANTIMACASSAR

A covering for the back or arms of an overstuffed chair or sofa to prevent soiling of the fabric, so named because originally used as a protection in the days when men used Macassar oil as hair dressing. In even earlier times bear's grease was in favor to give the male that well groomed look, this being replaced by Macassar oil when Yankee ships began trading with the East Indies after the Revolution.

Made from a tropical bean, the oil came from the Macassar region of Celebes, a large island lying due east of Borneo. In the Macassar Strait, the passage between these two islands, was fought in the early days of World War II, the famous night action between a Japanese convoy and four old destroyers of our Asiatic Fleet; a spectacular victory resulting in the destruction of a number of enemy transports. The antimacassars of early days were finely worked pieces of crocheting, with many varied designs, valued by antiquarians and widely imitated today.

BACKHOUSE

 A small wooden building in the rear of a dwelling house, sometimes attached, but more often at a short distance down a tree shaded path. This humble building has been the subject of innumerable jests, all of them exhibiting an unfortunate lack of appreciation of the fundamental usefulness of the backhouse. Indeed, one droll fellow went so far as to write a book on the subject and sold a million copies. A person with any historical perspective whatever realizes, of course, that plumbing as we know it today is one of man's most recent advances and the odoriferous edifice in the back yard, now practically gone from the American scene, was itself a great advance, did duty through the centuries and therefore deserves a modicum of respect. As to technical details, it should be noted that a backhouse in the best Nineteenth Century tradition had a crescent or a heart cut in the door, an extraordinarily flourishing trumpet vine growing over the outside of the structure, two orifices inside upon which adults might sit and one or more small orifices for children. A mail order catalogue hanging inside, a book of an uplifting nature on a shelf and a bucket of ashes and a scoop setting on the floor completed the arrangements. There are instances of "three holers," but the two orifice backhouse was standard. While a "one holer" was better than nothing, it failed to provide for the situation where two members of the household received simultaneous calls. A variety of other names used to be applied to this building, but failed to find general acceptance.

BAKER'S CART

A light wagon from which the old time baker peddled his wares from door to door. He had a harder time of it than the modern purveyor of bakery goods, for in an earlier day a housewife considered the use of "boughten" bread a confession of failure on her part. As for commercially made cake, the family would certainly have been made to go without dessert before she would have allowed such an article on the table. However, over the years, the baker and his cart gradually acquired new customers. A story is told of a little shaver in the fishing town of Marblehead, where children learn deep water language very early. Trotting down the path to his mother who was trading with the baker, he said, "Maw, don't buy crackers. Buy pie. We'll eat the guts and throw the shell to hell, gol durn it." To him a pie seemed like a marine creature, a crustacean, and he cared no more for the crust than he did for a piece of lobster shell.

BANKER

A fishing schooner working the Grand Banks; an 80 fathom shoal extending 500 miles southeast from Newfoundland that is one of the most productive fisheries in the entire world. Most of these vessels, two masters, hailed from Marblehead, Gloucester and Cape Cod, although many another port on the Yankee Coast sent schooners after the rich fare of codfish. The crews of a "banker" had to be rugged men; able blue water sailors and good dory men as

8

well, for much of their work was tending the trawl lines. Whatever the weather, rain or shine, heavy seas or a fog so thick a steamship could loom up out of the mist and run down a small boat without ever knowing it, the dories were lowered over the side and the men went out to take the cod off the hooks along the trawl line and set fresh bait. Back aboard the schooner with the day's catch, all hands turned to and cleaned the fish, salted them and stowed them below in the hold. All seafaring nations of the Western World have fished the Grand Banks from a time long before Columbus and they continue to do so today. For New England the cod fisheries have always been of basic economic importance; a lot of salt cod goes into the building of a true Yankee, every old-time merchant in these parts included it in his cargoes, present day Boston and Gloucester are two of the world's great fishing ports. So vital a factor is the codfish that a carved wooden likeness of him hangs in the Massachusetts House of Representatives. The Grand Banks fishermen, their schooners and their dories are immortalized in Kipling's classic "Captains Courageous."

BEAMSTER

An old time tannery worker whose job was to take each hide as it came from the lime vat, lay it over a rounded beam and with a curved knife scrape off the remaining hair. His was a malodorous task, for the lime and other chemicals and the raw hides going through the tanning process produced a vast and overpowering stench. No matter how much the beamster scrubbed himself after he got home, the pervasive odor remained with him and if he went to a church supper in the evening, or a lodge meeting, people gradually edged away from him. In the old days folks in tannery towns like Peabody and Salem and Woburn and Lynn had a ready explanation for the fact that when Nebuchadnezzar hove Daniel into the lion's den, the lions did not eat him. Daniel, they said, was a beamster.

BELL BUOY

A floating beacon anchored at a submerged reef, shoal or rock in navigable inshore waters. Upon a wide hollow steel cylinder is mounted a pyramid shaped frame, and in the frame is mounted a bell. The waves keep the structure in constant motion so the bell is never silent and it is a constant warning to mariners at night or in thick weather. No one who has been to sea, even in an excursion boat, can ever forget the mournful tolling of a bell buoy in the fog, at first distant and sepulchral, clearer and sharper as the vessel draws abeam of it, giving it a wide berth, then fainter in the white, blank wall of mist astern, a ghostly, faraway sound from a danger that is past.

BELLY BUMP

Riding a sled on a downhill run lying flat on the stomach. On an ordinary hill this does not provide any extra excitement, but if there are any knolls or rises that are at all sharp, or perhaps a small ski jump, the boy who slides this way will have a time of it. Many a lad has had the wind knocked out of him sliding belly bump, although he soon recovers under the Spartan treatment administered by his playmates. A girl who slides downhill belly bump is forthwith classified a tomboy.

BIG STICK

The fireman's term for his aerial ladder, the most valuable and handy piece of equipment in the department. Its base rests on a turntable on the frame of the truck, its hoisting device is hydraulic, mechanical, or compressed air. Rolling up to a burning building, the big stick is raised in seconds, the extension reaches out, the turntable moves the ladder to the exact point where needed and firemen go monkeying up to rescue whoever may be trapped by the fire. So versatile is this ladder that the men at the base can move it from one window to another with firemen still on it, thus effecting several rescues in quick succession. Life saving comes early, often before the engine companies get water on the fire, and many a medal is won by the laddermen. After the rescues, the big stick is used for less spectacular tasks, ventilating the roof, taking hose lines to upper floors, directing a stream from its "ladder pipe" at some high point. Yet most of the truck company's duty is done without using the big stick at all. They carry shorter ladders and innumerable tools, they are the workhorses of the department, chopping and ripping so the engine men can get water to the seat of the blaze. To them falls the dirty, sooty work of the "overhaul," when the fire is practically out, to see that no lingering spark sets it all ablaze again. The Hayes Aerial of 1870 was the first big stick. Today no first class fire department would be without its full quota of aerial ladders.

BLACK AS THE KING OF HELL'S RIDING BOOTS

The old rooster who first said this might have said "black as your hat" or "black as the ace of spades." And it is doubtless true that he had never seen the Old Nick, nor did he have any way of knowing whether he owned a pair of riding boots. Although based on inaccurate information and having the fault of an undue prolixity, the expression nevertheless gained currency among those who feel that unadorned similes are very tedious indeed.

BONE DISH

A narrow, curved dish meant to fit close to a dinner plate, its purpose being to provide a place of disposal for bones and other inedible bits. In the Nineteenth Century a really fine set of china always included bone dishes. This refinement seems to have died out with the passage of time.

BOSTON BAKED BEANS

The main course of Saturday night supper in New England since time immemorial, a hearty meal rich in protein and a favorite any day of the week in lumber camps and duck blinds. Put the beans to soak Friday night; early Saturday morning put them in the pot with $\frac{1}{2}$ cup sugar, 3 tablespoons of molasses, a teaspoon of salt, some dry mustard, a medium sized onion and a piece of lean salt pork on top, cover with water, put in a slow oven and let them bake and sizzle all day, adding water from time to time. Any good cook will tell you this recipe is no good and promptly come up with her own. Many people used to take their pot of beans to the baker early in the morning and let them stay in his big oven all day, calling for them just before supper. With the beans serve brownbread, ketchup, piccalilli, and be sure to have apple pie for dessert. Sunday morning breakfast is, of course, beans warmed over in the black iron spider. A pot of beans used to be a handy item to take to someone nearby who needed a little help, and old Aunt Myra had a pot every Saturday from each of three neighbors. She saw to it the beans carried her pretty well through the week. It isn't everybody who could handle such a diet, but Aunt Myra lived alone, which made it easier.

BOUGHT HIS THUMB

This one belongs with the remarks about sugar stretched out with sand, well watered milk, sawdust in the coffee and wooden nutmegs. When an old timer said "I bought his thumb" he meant that he suspicioned the storekeeper rested his thumb on the scales when weighing the meat or cheese or turnips, a procedure good for two or three more ounces on the dial and a few cents more on the price. A suggestion of this sort from the buyer usually started an acrid exchange of remarks satisfying to the participants and edifying to everyone else in the store.

BOUGHTEN BEANS

The housewife of a day now gone thus referred contemptuously to the inferior variety of baked beans compounded by professionals and purveyed to an undiscriminating public for mere money. She felt that any woman so indolent as to neglect to give her family a Saturday night supper made with her own hands according to her own recipe was indeed a slack mortal. Possibly she might yield to the extent of sending Tommy down to the local bakery Friday night with her potful, so they could go in the big oven along with dozens of the pots of neighbors, but she insisted that what her family ate must have what she thought to be the right amount of mustard, molasses, pork and an onion, with all the beans standing right side up. However, the professionals have won out, boughten beans in cans are almost universal, with a great saving of time and probably possessing most of the vigor of old time beans baked at home, although many a Yankee feels that with the modern method there is a note missing.

BRASS MONKEY

A creature which suffers to an unusual degree in our severe New England winters. When the glass is near zero and the northwest wind is piercing, people say, "It's cold enough to freeze the tail off a brass monkey." Occasionally on a particularly bad winter day some more imaginative fellow fancies that other parts of this animal are affected by the cold. A few have seen the Vermont panther, or his tracks, but those who say they have seen the brass monkey generally change their story in the morning.

BREAKERS AHEAD

A warning phrase often used in speaking to one whose course of conduct is leading him into a dangerous situation. Originally this was a cry in the night from the masthead lookout on a sailing ship when from his lofty perch he saw angry white water in the darkness ahead. Immediately he hailed the deck in a salt water bellow that had every ounce of wind he could summon. The officer on watch, knowing he was heading for a ledge, or a submerged rock, or possibly the shore itself, immediately gave the command to the man at the wheel to put the helm hard down to port or to starboard, whichever side he judged to have the best water. When such a cry echoed the length of the ship, the watch below generally tumbled out, the master came on deck, and no one really breathed easy until the ship bore away from the

menace ahead. Then the officers took their bearings anew, squinted at the chart and tried to figure out how they came so near to having a close look into Davy Jones' locker. The master of the ship, if he was any good, tried to find out why the officer who had the deck came to lose his bearings, and asked him some mighty uncomfortable questions.

BRIDLE CHAIN

Used in lumbering operations in winter to wrap around the runners of the log sled to act as a brake when it came down the mountain loaded. The chain dug into the snow of the cart road, holding the sled back somewhat. Occasionally the chain parted or slipped off, the sled gained momentum on its glass smooth runners and the horses, sensing their danger, would break into a downhill run to keep ahead of the heavy load. If one horse stumbled, down he went, and so did his mate, the sled went over them and the lumber operator would have to send for a new span and perhaps a new driver. In the north country, where someone had lumbered the side of the mountain, one could sometimes see the skeletons of a few horses at the foot of a steep pitch in the cart road. Careful operators saw to it they rigged snub lines at the top of each steep slope. From the rear of the log sled a stout rope ran to a big tree, a half a dozen turns were taken around the base of the trunk and a man was posted there to pay out the line as the load went downhill. This gave real control. On old logging roads one can see trees and big stumps that have been used to anchor snub lines; deeply grooved by the pressure and friction of ropes under the tremendous stress of a load of green saw timber going down the mountain.

BRINDLE

The heavy dictionary says this is a state of color having dark streaks or spots on a gray or tawny background. Old timers were not so specific; they used it to describe any dark color defying exact classification. Most often it referred to a cow showing no trace of any known breed; the descendant of a long line of scrub bulls and mere "cow" cows. When applying the adjective to some dark color not at all attractive, such as a paint job where remains from several pots had been mixed and used, the word brindle was often preceded by an earthy monosyllabic word which has always emphasized complete disapproval.

BROOK PASSAGE

Many of us, driving along a winding country road, have wondered why it is we so often see beside the little bridge over a brook a loop in the road leading off the highway, down through the bed of the stream and up the slope again to rejoin the main thoroughfare. If we pause to look carefully, two ruts are plainly visible and the bed of the sedge lined brook at this point is flat without large stones. Even in this day of motor cars we might see in the soft earth the wheel tracks of a buggy or wagon and the hoof marks of a horse. We wonder why, with a perfectly good bridge at hand, anyone would be so bemused as to drive his horse and buggy through the water. The reason is an excellent one, going back to a time long before the internal combustion engine was ever thought of. In hot dry weather a horse's hooves tend to become dry and brittle. The rims of the wheels and the spokes, over dry, are likely to shrink and loosen; a process which, if long continued, may result

18

in the situation in which the Deacon found himself when his famous One Hoss Shay at last gave out. So the old timers seized every opportunity to moisten hooves, rims and spokes, take a short rest in the cool shade, light a pipe or bite off a chew of tobacco. The brook passage was used only in summer. In Spring, when it carried off the excess water from a sodden landscape and in the Fall after the Line Storm, it was a raging torrent. At such times drivers stayed on the road, counting themselves fortunate if they got over it without being mired.

BRUSH HARROW

Constructed by cutting eight or ten small birch trees and nailing them to a six foot length of two by four timber. (Note: use twenty penny nails). A stout hook is screwed into the middle of the two by four, the whiffletree is hitched on and the harrow is ready for the farmer to use in brushing into the ground the hay or grain seed just sowed on the freshly prepared field. Covered with earth, the seeds are protected from the crows and sparrows. Best to pull a brush harrow is an old black horse who takes his time, likes his work and generally improves the soil a little as he plods up and down. The brush harrow does not appear in the catalogues of most farm implement companies.

BUCKET OF STEAM

One of the things the old hands were likely to send a lad to get on his first day at work in the shop.

If he actually asked for it at the supply room, he was likely to be told next day to go draw a can of striped paint or a left handed monkey wrench or a spool of pipe thread. In a printer's office he would be requested to examine closely an article already set in type, and tied with string to see if he could find any "type lice" in it. Usually the humorist who promoted this one had watered the type and would squeeze the block while the boy searched for the lice, sending an inky spray into his face. It is more difficult to bamboozle the youth of today with such crude jokes, perhaps because they have viewed so many professional funny men on television and in the movies that they have seen everything and heard everything.

BUTCHER CART

Another of the tradesmen's vehicles which called at the door in the days before automobiles, good roads and supermarkets. The housewife would select her meat order from what the butcher had hanging in his wagon and he would cut it on a massive wooden block with his cleaver, weigh it on scales suspended from one of the struts of his canvas topped vehicle and wrap it for her, unless she had brought out a plate. Meat did not come in refrigerator cars from the big mid-west packing houses, as it does today. The butcher not only did a door-to-door selling job over a route sometimes extending miles into the rural regions; he often slaughtered his meat on his own premises, performing every step in the procedure of turning a live animal into various merchantable cuts ranging from sirloin steak for the well-to-do, to liver and lights for the folks who were struggling to make both ends meet. Cowhides he sold to the tanneries, bones to the rendering works and what had no other value ended up in the fertilizer factory. Considerable commotion attended the slaughtering operations of the local butcher and anyone who has ever been within a half mile of a pig sticking will never forget it. Sometimes, when a North Country butcher had a day off, he took his gun and went deer hunting and if he was lucky his business had an extra dividend. The venison he generally renamed for the trade and it was usually lamb by the time the ultimate consumer had a look at it.

BUTTON UP FOR THE WINTER

In the country this consists of many important steps; storm windows and storm doors; long narrow bags of sand to lay on the window sills and on the tops of the lower sashes to keep the north wind from whistling through the joints; a woodshed full packed with oak, beech, birch and maple and a hefty pile in the yard to begin on; a fence of light boards a foot away from the foundation of the house and reaching sill high, the space in between filled with dry leaves and hay to keep the cold air from working into the cellar; a mulch of straw and such around the young fruit trees and over the strawberry bed and the perennials in the flower garden. If any new stove pipes are needed, it is well to see to them before snow flies and if the roof needs any work, better get up there before Thanksgiving Day and attend to it. Be sure there are enough canned goods on the shelves to feed the family during one of those three day blizzards when there is not a wheel turning and enough grain in the barn so a quick trip into town is never necessary if the stock is to be fed. When all these details are taken care of, dig up the long underwear and shake the mothballs out of them and put them on the line for an airing. Then relax and try to think what spring will be like.

CALLIOPE

The musical instrument fetching up the rear of the old time circus parade. Installed on a heavy wagon drawn by ten horses, the calliope itself was a bank of king size organ pipes or, more often, a set of steam whistles tuned to the notes of the musical scale. At the back a colored man shoveled coal into the firebox of a vertical steam boiler; up ahead, behind the drivers box, sat a man in a blue uniform ready to go to work at his keyboard when the guage beside his sheet music told him he had steam pressure enough. The calliope was beautiful to hear at a distance from a quarter mile to three miles; far away, haunting tones like the sound of the express whistling for a crossing somewhere up the valley. As soon as the parade left the circus field, small boys

22

in school commenced to wriggle restlessly in their seats at the sound of the calliope's distant notes in soft spring air. School always recessed as the parade drew near and one of the high points was that moment at the end when the man at the keyboard shuffled his sheet music and gave with a tune. Steam spurted from the row of whistles, the song blasted tremendously forth, the boys figured it was just about loud enough, the girls covered their ears and every driver made sure to be at his horse's head, a firm hand on the bridle. And then the parade was gone, the smell of the calliope's soft coal smoke lingering, a mellower tune floating back from blocks away. The children reluctantly returned to school and, when they had settled down, the teacher would explain that the "steam piano" is named calliope for one of the Greek muses, the mother of Orpheus, a fellow who made much more refined music on a stringed instrument. But the boys still had their ears cocked for another tune done in steam.

CANDLEMAS DAY

The feast of the purification of the Virgin Mary, celebrated on February second. In some churches the candles are blessed on this day. The farmers of an earlier time had a rhyme, "Candlemas Day, half your wood, and half your hay," which meant that it is the midpoint of winter, and they could look at their lofts and their woodpiles and get a fairly good idea of whether they were going to make it.

(See Groundhog Day)

23

CAPE COD TURKEY

A phrase to describe salt cod, invented by some fellow who believed in making the best of things. The old time Yankee knew what turkey tasted like, but after he had stretched out the Thanksgiving bird to the final wishbone soup a week later, it was more likely to be salt cod that he ate regularly. In these parts, cod are much cheaper to raise and easier to keep. Most families kept a king size salt cod hanging by its tail on the wall of the shed, well out of the way of both the cat and the mice. The lady of the house would hack off a piece, put it to soak, and serve it with boiled potatoes and beets, with perhaps an egg sauce if there was company for supper.

CAPTAIN'S WALK

A small platform, fenced in, set upon the highest point on the roof of a house in a New England seaport town. The walk, reached by a trap door from the attic, provided the retired sea captain, who had become a merchant, with a position from which he could command a view of the harbor and the waters beyond. When one of his ships was due he would be striding up and down his walk, pausing frequently to have another look with his telescope, and if no ship of his was expected, nevertheless he was likely to be aloft with his glass, for no true mariner loses interest in what is going on at sea until it is time to lay him away.

(See "Widow's Walk")

CHEMICAL ENGINE

A piece of fire apparatus widely used in the latter half of the 19th and early part of the 20th century. It carried two large tanks full of a solution of bicarbonate of soda and at the top of each tank a bottle of sulphuric acid. In boxes or on reels were two lines of one inch hose. At the fire the bottles of sulphuric acid were inverted and a chemical reaction took place producing carbon dioxide gas, the pressure of which forced out streams that easily reached the roof of a small house. It was ideal for fighting inside fires where it was sought to avoid the water damage caused by heavy lines. In a big fire, the chemical engine patrolled the area downwind, ready to extinguish any roof ignited by sparks, and it carried a short ladder for that purpose. In outlying districts a chemical was often the only engine, its mission being to hold the fire until a steamer and hose wagon could gallop out from one of the downtown stations. Some communities with no water supply maintained a chemical in the hope it could check the fire while still small. Sometimes it turned out this way, but when the tanks were empty, this engine was done until it could get more water, soda and acid. Besides the "straight chemical," most cities had "combinations," a piece of kit carrying smaller tanks and about 800 feet of big hose with which to lay a hydrant line. Chemical tanks were carried on some ladder trucks and motor pumps. Except for the $2\frac{1}{2}$ gallon "sody and acid" extinguisher, a familiar

25

sight to everyone, the chemical is now obsolete. A large water tank and a motor "booster" pump does the work, usually as an auxiliary unit on a regular engine or ladder truck; occasionally as a separate tank outfit with capacity as high as 1000 gallons for use in rural areas.

CHIMBLEY

The accepted pronunciation of the word appearing in standard dictionaries as *chimney*. *Chimley* is of frequent enough occurrence to have become an authorized alternate pronunciation.

CHUNKWOOD

In the days when air tight stoves were an important factor in keeping a house anywhere near liveable in a New England winter, the prudent Yankee classified his fire wood with great care. In the shed he kept dry pine for kindling, and arm size sticks of oak, birch, beech and maple to keep the room warm enough to sit in of a January evening. This fuel would do it even in the full of the moon with the northwest wind hurrying down from Hudson's Bay and the glass below zero, if he kept the lower draft open and tossed another stick into the firebox every little while. But at bed time different fuel was required if the fire was to keep even enough to have a few coals in the stove by morning. For this he had saved chunkwood; big pieces of oak and elm full of knots and so tough even Hercules could not split

26

them with his axe. Into the stove went an assortment of these, with perhaps a few roots he had grubbed up, or a piece from the crotch of a tree, until the firebox was full. Then the dampers were closed tight, every one hustled off to bed and these heavy pieces mulled through the night. In the morning, if the chunkwood had been carefully selected, the room was above freezing and at the bottom of the stove were glowing coals hot enough to get an armful of wood going merrily when the drafts were opened. This is the day of the thermostat and the Yankee need no longer keep an eye open for chunkwood to serve him well in January.

CHURCH STICK

In Colonial days when the minister who could deal with sin and damnation in less than an hour was a rarity, many church goers had a tendency to snooze a bit except when the preacher was making the flames really roll up from hell. The deacons took care of this by providing the tithing man with a light staff, on one end of which was a rabbit's foot and on the other a foxtail. He patrolled the aisles, tickled the chin of anyone who had fallen asleep and if the man woke up with an ejaculation inappropriate to the time and place, the tithing man held his finger to his lips to still any unseemly levity.

CIDER

The juice of the apple, its quality depending upon what man does to it after the grinding and pressing process. *Store Cider* has been strained and bottled and pasteurized or has a tiny bit of chemical additive to keep it from doing what comes naturally. *Rotten apple* cider has undergone a minimum of tampering, it is everything that comes from the squeezing of the heterogeneous mixture of apples shoveled from the truck into the grinder, it has body, no chemicals, it has worked a little and a glass from the spigot at the mill is a real drink. Better still a glassful from the jug after it has popped the cork a few times, but do not forget your jug and come back ten days later, for the working will have continued and it will be either vinegar or a horrid and sludgy mess. *Russet cider* made carefully and from quality apples is expensive, but worth every cent it costs. *Hard Cider* starts with sweet cider and, guided by an expert through various stages, becomes a really terrific potation. A Yankee farmer on a winter evening in his kitchen listening to the blizzard howl around the house and pile deep drifts against his buildings has no difficulty, after a few hookers of this stuff, in imagining that the Arctic gale is a tropic zephyr gently filling the topsails of his ship as it approaches the palm fringed beach of some South Sea Isle, where coconuts and breadfruit and lithe brown skinned maidens await him and his men, weary with long months at sea.

CISTERN

A tank to hold water in storage for household use, varying in capacity from a half barrel to a reservoir holding thousands of gallons. Some are in the cellar with the rain spouts connected, so the drainage from the roof flows in. This arrangement provides an ample supply of soft water for washing; a great convenience when the well water is so "hard" that soap will not lather in it. For fire protection many towns had enormous cisterns beneath the streets, fed by springs or by pipes leading from ponds at a distance. Their use has been gradually abandoned as water mains have been perfected and extended. Some country folks have a cistern beside the kitchen sink, with water piped from a spring. One ingenious Yankee had a 20 gallon crock for a cistern in his kitchen and a pipe bent over to serve as a faucet. The stream in the pipe had to be allowed to run constantly to prevent freeze-ups, but his wife, for personal reasons, did not like the continual sound of running water. He bored a hole in a cork, inserted a goose quill and tied a string on the end of it, so the water would dribble noiselessly down into the crock. Another hole was drilled in the crock three inches below the top and a pipe inserted which carried the overflow to the cattle tub outside the kitchen door. Such water as the stock did not drink overflowed from the tub and was wasted, except in so far as it helped keep the grass in the backyard green in dry spells.

(See Trout in the Well)

CLAMBAKE

A tremendous feed, a social event, a ritual, the proper details of which are acridly disputed among numerous Yankee bakemasters, amateur and professional. The usual procedure is to dig a shallow hole, line it with stones, build a roaring wood fire, feed it for two hours until it thoroughly heats the stones, then rake it. A layer of seaweed is placed on the hot stones, then the clams, and another thick layer of seaweed. A piece of an old topsail (although a jib will do) is laid over it all and kept wet and the whole business steams while everyone swaps yarns. After two hours, off comes sailcloth and the seaweed, and it is time to eat. If the clambake is in charge of a real virtuoso and there is plenty of money, there may be lobster, chicken, hot dogs, corn on the cob and potatoes, a feed fit for a New Englander or a dweller upon Olympus. A clambake may be small in a barrel size hole for a family group or any larger size, according to the multitude to be fed. Details, such as the thickness of the layers of the seaweed and the time of steaming, vary according to what tradition the bakemaster has had handed down to him from those original Yankees, the Abenaki Indians, for they are the originators of this feast.

CLAWING OFF A LEE SHORE

This phrase, coming to us from the days of sail, refers to the struggles of any one in serious difficulties. When a sailing ship was near the coast and the wind changed, blowing her toward the land, the skipper was obliged to sail against the wind, (beat to windward), or be blown ashore and wrecked. The shore, being down wind, was to the lee of the ship, hence the term "lee shore." Beating to windward is slow, tedious and difficult even in the open sea, and when it must be managed by a crew who can look over their shoulders as they work ship and see the foaming white of breakers on the rocks, it is a terrifying experience. If the ship was able to beat to windward and make headway against the adverse wind (i.e. a wind foul for her course), she would make the open sea and safety. But if the wind was too strong and she was blown toward the lee shore and if, when she dropped her anchors, they dragged and did not hold, then she drove onto the rocks and struck, and the beachcombers had rich pickings in the morning. So difficult was the maneuver of working against a strong wind when near the shore, that it was termed "clawing off."

CLIPPER SHIP

The ultimate acheivement of marine architects in the days of sail, developed in New York and Boston yards in the few years following 1850. The principles had been known for years; especially among Chesapeake Bay builders, yet the clipper never came to full flower as a deep sea carrier until the California Gold Rush caused freight rates to rise sky high. The clipper had a sharp concave bow, a sharp stern, she was longer in proportion to her beam, had longer spars, both upper and lower topsails, skysails for a little extra speed in light airs and studding sails extending beyond the regular sails to catch any vagrant puff of wind in a tropic calm. Donald McKay of Boston led them all as a builder, closely followed by the New Yorkers. With ships like *Flying Cloud, Lightning, Westward Ho* and *Sovereign of the Seas,* records around Cape Horn to Frisco and on the Atlan-

tic crossing were broken again and again. The run of the *James Baines*, Boston to Liverpool, in 12 days and 6 hours was something none of the primitive steamships of that day could approach and as for a voyage around the Horn, no steamer had the coal capacity to attempt it. Yet steam, little more than a quarter century old, continued to develop and little time was to pass before the propellor driven vessel put an end to the glorious clippers and their hell driving skippers who never left the deck when there was an extra ounce of speed to be coaxed out of the ship. The steamer took over the important ocean runs, no more clippers were built and of those that were afloat many ended as coal boats. It is important to note that "clipper" means the speedy and specially designed ship of the mid-Nineteenth Century and not just any square rigger. The Yankee ships that made New England ports rich after the Revolution were not clippers, but heavier, wider, bluff bowed craft with nowhere near the sail area of the clipper. In fact, but one clipper ever entered the harbor of Salem, which in the early Nineteenth Century was one of the busiest ports in the world, but which had lapsed into relative unimportance by the time this marine masterpiece had been evolved.

COLD CELLAR

A room in the cellar of an old time house for storage of foods that needed to be kept in a cool place. Usually it was separated from the rest of the cellar by a stone or brick wall or sometimes a wooden partition, thus preventing the circulation of air and maintaining a lower temperature in warm weather. Later, when central heating systems came into use, with furnaces in the cellar, it was even more important to have this storage room walled off. Here were stored apples and pears, the root vegetables such as potatoes, turnips, carrots packed in sand, beets and parsnips. A crock with cooking eggs put down in waterglass and a barrel of salt pork or salt beef, were kept here and shelves lined with jars of preserves; crab apple jelly, pickled pears, plum jam, and the forty eleven varieties of "sass" a good wife managed to concoct over her hot kitchen stove during the good weather months. Fresh food at the stores was not available to anywhere near the extent that it is today, canned goods were not common until well into the 19th century and there was no such thing as a deep freeze unit this side of the Arctic Circle. No refrigeration existed other than that provided by the ice man or, on the farm, such ice as was cut from the pond in winter and packed in sawdust in a little structure in the yard in the hope it would last pretty well through the summer. So every other means of preserving food was used as much as possible.

COMPOST HEAP

The pile into which every prudent gardner throws all his cuttings, thinnings, grass clippings and old stalks. Although any vegetable matter will do, the frugal folks up this way save cigar butts and all the pea pods, corn husks, potato parings and other residuum usually consigned to the garbage can. The dry leaves of autumn should always be included. While it is more fun to burn them, it has been estimated that the annual fall of leaves on an ordinary place are equal in plant food value to a one dollar bag of fertilizer. To the heap are added any other near at hand items that are likely to help the garden grow; indeed, a couple of otherwise respectable suburbanites nearly came to blows in a dispute over which had prior claim to the "dressing" left in the street by the milkman's horse. The resulting pile of refuse has aptly been termed "garden hash." After a year or so of dampness and rotting, with occasional sprinklings of lime, this variegated mixture becomes black loam of the finest quality, fertile topsoil that will do wonders for any garden or lawn. And it does not cost a cent.

CONCORD FIGHT

The expression many old timers use in referring to the Battle of Concord and Lexington, April 19, 1775, when the American Minute Men fought the red coated British Regulars. "The shot heard'round the world" was fired on Lexington Green early in the morning, only the local militia being involved. As word spread to the north and west and south, the patriots came streaming in from every village and farm to join in the fight that raged from Concord Bridge all the way back to the Charles River. Every town within a fifty mile radius had men who were there to take a shot at the King's troops from behind a tree or stonewall. So to this day old timers around Boston, upon meeting a friend, say: "Where you been? I haven't seen you since the Concord Fight." The lustre of this famous victory, kept bright by those whose ancestors swapped hot lead with the British, has in no wise been dimmed by the Irish among us.

CORN HUSK MATTRESS

Easy to make from materials ready at hand, it was common among the less affluent, and in the old days that included nearly everyone. Serving well folks who worked hard and slept soundly, it had the advantage that it could be acquired without signing promissory notes, having one's credit looked up or entering into any instalment payment arrangements. For moderns who are accustomed to sleeping on the inner spring masterpieces of today's sleeping engineers, a night up country on one of the old corn husk jobs is a memorable experience. The husks rustle every time the bed's occupant turns, the thing in uneven, a few cobs put in there to give the mattress body are likely to stick into some sensitive part of one's anatomy. If a mouse who has made his home somewhere amongst the cobs and husks starts to gnaw in the middle of the night, a city fellow is likely to throw the whole business out of the window and finish the night on the floor.

CRANBERRY JUNCTION

The station in Carver, Massachusetts where one boards the Edaville Railroad for a five and a half mile ride around the vast cranberry bogs of the Atwood plantation. The railroad is a two foot guage, the rolling stock and engines came from the old Bridgeton & Harrison line in Maine. The locomotives are coal fired steam jobs with king-sized whistles that blow for every one of the many grade crossings. On the way back they give two blasts at a fixed point in memory of Ellis D. Atwood, the founder. Far out in the bogs in Edaville is the one stop on this little line, where everyone detrains for a chicken and cranberry barbecue under the pines, a look at the collection of old locomotives and cars, antique auto-

mobiles, and the railroad and fire engine museums, and the kids get a ride on a modern motor fire engine. The place is unique in that the operation of some of the cranberry bogs, important in the economy of southeastern Massachusetts, is combined with the display of so many Yankee antiquities, including steam locomotives in active use.

CUP PLATE

A small flat plate not quite the diameter of the cup itself, used to set the cup on after the tea or coffee had been poured into the saucer for cooling. The saucer that went with an old fashioned tea cup was deeper than those used today, more like what we call a fruit or cereal dish. It was perfectly good table manners to pour the tea into the saucer, and, when it cooled a bit, to drink it from the saucer. The cup plate was a refinement, something to set the cup on so that any moisture on the bottom would not stain the table cloth. Some were made of Sandwich glass, works of art and now highly prized by collectors. The story is told of a lady riding in a stage coach who went into an inn to have a cup of coffee while the horses were being changed. It was served so hot that she feared it would not cool in the few minutes allowed the passengers for refreshments. A wagon man sitting nearby, seeing her dilemma, said, "Here, lady, take mine. It's all saucered an' blowed."

CURFEW

As recently as the early part of this century, the bells in New England steeples tolled at nine in the evening as a warning to all children to be off the streets, although few heeded it. In olden days it was required that everyone be in his house at curfew, or, as old timers phrased it, "honest men should be in bed and rascals on their way home." In the eighties and nineties young people started home at curfew, although some were breaking away from this strict rule. To those who started home the more independent ones would say "Are you still tied to the bell rope?" In some present day towns, where the juvenile delinquency problem becomes acute, curfew is enforced for a while until conditions become stabilized. The rule is also enforced in enemy countries under occupation, so that the conquering army may more easily control the subject population. The word comes from the French couvre-feu, referring to the medieval rule that all fires must be covered or extinguished at a certain hour in the evening.

CUT OF HIS JIB

A nautical phrase that has come ashore; now widely used to mean a man's appearance, manner and way of doing things. When we say of a man we do not "like the cut of his jib," we mean that viewed from a distance he creates an unfavorable impression. In the days of sailing ships, each vessel had minor peculiarities in the arrangement of its canvas and rigging; differences sufficient to make of each ship an individual. A ship master, standing on the quarterdeck with his telescope to his eye, would first try to identify a faraway ship by carefully examining its sails and rigging. The jib, one of the headsails, a triangular canvas easy to pick out at a distance, was one of the first features of a strange ship to be noted. If it was cut in a manner peculiar to the British navy or the French privateers or the Mediterranean corsairs, the skipper would say "I don't like the cut of her jib" and immediately he would give orders to change his vessel's course so he would not be obliged to have any closer acquaintance with this ominous looking stranger. But if he did like the cut of her jib, he would steer a course to come up with her, bring his ship to and speak her. Fore topsails aback to check headway, the two captains would bellow news to each other through their speaking trumpets. They might even lay to long enough to swap provisions, do a little trading and let the crews gossip a bit and try their hands at cheating each other in the exchange of the small items a sailor always has in his sea chest.

DAOWN BUCKET

 A Marbleheader thus greets a friend. Whether he meets him walking along the street, or sees him driving by in a car or working on a nearby wharf or repairing a motor on some boat out in the harbor, the cry is the same. And the reply is always "up for air." Some think that "daown bucket" originated aboard the fishing vessels as a warning when the men on deck lowered away to those working below. Others claim it is a warning shouted by a housewife when she emptied from an upper bedroom window a receptacle she should have taken out to the backyard. This warning was desirable in a town where so many houses are built right up to the street line and anything tossed out of a window may strike a pedestrian in the head. Elementary courtesy required that the pedestrian be given adequate notice of what the lady was about to do. A lady who omitted this formality might hear the crash of glass as an outraged passerby let fly a rock or two at her front windows.

DARTMOUTH COLLEGE

Located at Hanover, New Hampshire on the east bank of the Connecticut River five miles above its confluence with the White River. Founded in 1769 by Rev. Eleazar Wheelock for the free education of Indians in the wilderness country but recently come under the dominion of the British by virtue of their victory in the French and Indian War, it was financed at first by Lord Dartmouth and other charitably minded Englishmen. White men are now admitted, but are obliged to pay. Although the school at present has considerable contact with the civilized world, its motto continues to be **"Vox Clamantis In Deserto,"** which means "A Voice Crying in the Wilderness."

DASHBOARD

A shield of heavy leather or light wood on supports of selected ash in front of the driver's seat on a buggy, surry or carryall. Most vehicles had nothing in front of the driver and he jogged along with a near view of the horse's rump, his ankles swished by the animal's tail whenever the flies on the after part of the critter became too pestiferous. The dashboard was a refinement for passenger vehicles, so that when the horse was at a smart trot, the choice assortment of mud and manure his hooves picked up from the unpaved road would not land in the laps of the riders. It had the further advantage of keeping the passengers in the vehicle if the horse stopped suddenly, for

otherwise they might pitch forward and fetch up on the ground under his hooves — a very dangerous place to be if he was having a bad day, and horses, like people, do have bad days. "Kicking the dashboard," a phrase that has come to us from those days, we use now to describe a person who is obstreperous and difficult, like a horse which refuses to go forward and is letting fly with his heels. Note that the first automobiles had dashboards, since they were no more than standard buggies with a putt-putt contraption under the seat and a tiller to steer with.

DECALCOMANIA

The art or process of transferring pictures or designs from specially prepared paper to china, glass or wood. Women who refinish old furniture are familiar with this method of placing the representation of a bunch of flowers or a basket of fruit on a chair back. Men well remember that in the little store near the schoolhouse where they generally stopped for a cent's worth of jelly beans, "baked beans," or chewing gum, a couple of gum drops or an acrid tasting chocolate peppermint, decalcomanias were for sale. The boys called them "stickers," they lapped them, transferred the pictures to the back of the hand or the forearm and admired the gaudy peach or plum or rose when they should have been listening to some fellow student try to parse a verb. The teacher had an eye out for boys who were playing with decalcomanias and when discovered she sent them to the "basement" to wash off the work of art and then told them they could stay after school for a while.

DEMOCRAT WAGON

A light, one horse vehicle with a flat bottom, narrow sides six inches high, a tail board, and two moveable seats that fitted onto the sides with U shaped pieces of strap iron. The seats could be slid back and forth along the sides or removed altogether. Thus the owner could use his wagon like a buggy, with a single seat, or he could fit in the second seat and take the whole family for a Sunday afternoon ride; mother in front with him and the children fussing and fighting in the rear. If he had a milk route, he could accommodate a few dozen bottles in the wagon, if he had to pick up some bags of grain at the store, it was just right, and for a small load of hay it was mighty handy as long as the driver walked alongside. The nearest thing to a Democrat wagon we have today is a pick-up truck, but that is not much of a vehicle for taking the family to ride.

DERNE STREET

A short thoroughfare at the rear of the State House in Boston named to commemorate a little known but glorious victory. In the war with Tripoli, General William Eaton of Brimfield, Massachusetts, one of the most fiery officers ever to wear the American uniform, organized an expedition in Egypt to march against Derne, the most eastern of the Bashaw's seaports. He had eight U. S. Marines, a company of valiant Greeks recruited in the Nile Valley and a horde of Tripolitan horsemen, followers of the exiled Hamet, who claimed to be the rightful Bashaw. Day after day Eaton marched across the sand and rock of North Africa with his rugged Marines and Greeks, using all his powers of diplomacy and persuasion to keep Hamet's irregular Tripolitan cavalrymen with him. When he reached the walls of Derne the U. S. Navy had the *Argus, Nautilus* and *Hornet* in the harbor, their batteries pounded the forts with round shot, while Eaton's Greeks manned their artillery pieces on the landward side. The walls were breached, and Eaton's army surged into the fortress to raise the American flag over the citadel. Peace with Tripoli soon followed and when Eaton returned to his native Massachusetts, he was received as a hero for his conquest of this Barbary stronghold five thousand miles from America's shores. The Legislature presented him with 10,000 acres of the "eastern lands" in what is now Aroostook County and to memorialize his hard won victory forever, Derne Street was given its name.

DEVIL'S DANCING ROCK

A wide flat stone the size of a table top or larger, worn smooth by glacial action, frequently found in

New England pastures or on a little knoll. It was a saying among the old settlers that in the full of the moon anyone who looked sharp might see the Old Scratch himself doing a solo dance on such a rock. Whoever saw him was well advised to hurry along.

DINOSAUR TRACKS

Found in the rock strata of the Connecticut River Valley here and there from Middletown to Greenfield, these footprints left by an earlier Yankee on the sands of time are now sold by thrifty land owners to those who desire a distinctive hearthstone in the new house or flagstones for the front walk that excite the curiosity of visitors. The many colleges of the valley all have in their museums and lecture halls specimens of these thin rock strata with dinosaur footprints to help the students understand that this world did not begin with them. It was in the Triassic Age, 150 million years ago, that the dinosaur, an enormous lizard 80 feet long, strode up and down the Connecticut Valley, leaving these marks. The wet sand over countless centuries hardened and became rock. Floods brought down silt and debris from upstream to cover this formation and it remained buried until our time, when ever curious man dug it up, and speculated about the nature of these enormous reptiles who lived here when New England had a hot and steaming climate. Fossilized bones have been found, the big footprints have been studied and scientists have formed an estimate of the size and shape of the great dinosaur, hulking along the river banks, sometimes dragging his enormous tail and leaving a mark as he browsed on the plentiful tropical vegetation that grew here in the days before one of a Yankee's chief concerns was the amount of his heating bill.

DOG BARKING NAVIGATOR

A mariner who steers a course near the coast so he may know his position by sighting lighthouses, buoys, islands, hills on shore and other landmarks. Generally a ship master who hugs the coast is poor at blue water navigation and would not be sure where he was if he were out of sight of land for long, so, not trusting his ability to use his sextant to "shoot the sun" and thereby ascertain his exact latitude and longitude, he relies heavily on frequent looks at familiar objects. Sailors love to use exaggerative expressions, and "dog barking navigator" is one such. The idea behind it is that this skipper judges his position by the individual peculiarites in the barking of dogs ashore with which he has become familiar as he has fumbled his way up and down the coast. Such a sea captain makes sailors uneasy, for they fear the dark night when he may listen to the wrong dog and pile his vessel up on a ledge or drive her ashore in the breakers. But let no one think a good mariner does not value the opportunity to take bearings on points ashore, however much fun he may make of the man who fears to sail the open sea.

The U. S. Government Pilot books, at the steerman's elbow in every ship, describes the beaches and mountains and hills and smokestacks and church steeples on every coast in the world with a particularity that would do credit to a travel agency folder. Even the characteristics of the trees and fields and dwellings are noted. Thus a captain, fog bound, who catches a glimpse of shore when the mists part for a few seconds, may recognize something mentioned in the pilot book open before him, whether he be off Cape Cod or Java Head or Finisterre, and lay his course accordingly.

DOLLOP

As much as the cook thinks is right.

DOLPHIN STRIKER

Sometimes called the Martingale, a strong spar at the end of the bowsprit, at a right angle to it and pointing downward, its function being to support the martingale stays running ahead to the jib boom and flying jib boom and, in the other direction, to the bow of the ship. The whole structure of dolphin striker and martingale stays formed a triangular truss-work of great strength on the underside of bowsprit, jib boom and flying jib boom. Since the upward pull exerted by the four headsails is tremendous when a stiff breeze is blowing, this strengthening on the underside is necessary to prevent the booms from being snapped like matchsticks. The dolphin striker is a prime example of the careful engineering that went into the design of a sailing ship. Its name the mariners gave it because dolphins love to play about the bow of a ship at sea, leaping gracefully from the water and escorting the vessel for miles. When the sea was rough and the vessel was pitching, this spar would plunge into the water and old sailors would tell a landsman aboard that sometimes it speared a dolphin and brought him up, flopping and struggling, so the cook might provide fresh fare for the before the mast hands.

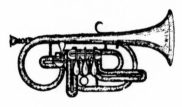

DOUBLE IN BRASS

Meaning the capability of performing two quite different functions in an organization, this idiom comes to us from the show world. In a small troupe of players, and sometimes in a large one, an actor worked away at the trumpet or tuba in the orchestra during the overture, then slipped backstage, glued on a black mustachio, strapped a pistol holster to his hip and shortly appeared before the footlights in time to beat Murgatroyd to the draw and save the fair heroine from a fate worse than death. At intermission he would be back in the orchestra pit, working hard. Doubling in brass was at its picturesque best in the circus, where men pounded tent stakes and raised canvas in the early morning and by parade time, clad in red or green or blue, were atop one of the wagons, ready to give with a wind instrument . These roustabout bands, some negro, some white, produced music unlike anything heard elsewhere, then or since. They were not the regular circus bands, but groups of six or eight on lesser wagons in the long parade. With slide trombone and thumping drum the black men managed to bring the spirit of darkest Africa to Main Street, while a little further down the parade, a group of Westerners played the songs of the cattle ranges to the throngs along the curbstones of the Yankee towns. Unfortunately no composer has ever caught for us the notes of the roustabout band.

DOWN ON HIS UPPERS

To be in poor circumstances and suffering a reversal of fortune. The upper is the part of the shoe above the sole, so a man who is down on his uppers is scuffing along with his bare feet practically on the ground, without the money to get his shoes tapped, let alone buy a new pair.

DRAGGING ANCHOR

The critical situation of a sailing ship whose skipper has dropped anchor so he may hold his position until the gale abates, only to find the anchor is not holding and his vessel is being blown toward the surf and the rocks. In common speech "dragging his anchor" is applied to a man who has lost control of

himself and is heading for trouble. If he is really inebriated, that regrettable condition is described as "three sheets in the wind, and dragging his anchor," which means he will sleep in the lockup and see the Judge in the morning.

DRY GOODS CART

In the days of the horse and buggy and dirt roads the dry goods man used to drive through the rural districts with his box-like light wagon carrying a choice of textiles no housewife could find short of Boston. The women watched for him and when his wagon drew up at the gate they were down the path before he was off the driver's seat. Letting down the back of his cart, he would display his bolts of cloth; calicos, muslins, ginghams, percales, or canvas, if anyone asked for it. Silk and fine laces were among his goods and if he did not have just what they fancied, he promised to have it next time around,

50

which might be months later, for such a route was a long one, — perhaps the entire reach of Cape Cod or winding over New Hampshire hill roads from the Merrimac to the Connecticut. When the dry goods man drove away from the lady's door, there were usually few coins left in the old teapot on the closet shelf, but enough cloth in her bureau drawer to keep her needle busy for many an evening. Some of these pedlars, diligent and eager to please, made tidy fortunes bringing quality merchandise to people in villages and on farms who, from one year's end to another, never saw anything but what was on the shelves of the general store.

EAST INDIA CAPTAIN

 A really top man in maritime New England in the days of sail, occupying an eminence which was the aspiration of every boy and meriting the respect of every adult. An East India Captain had to be good. He sailed forth with a ship carrying a fortune, he was responsible for the safety of vessel and crew on the long voyage around the Cape of Good Hope and through the Indian Ocean with its violent tropical weather and prowling piratical craft. Getting a ship up river to Calcutta required skill, yet greater skill was required when he reached port to trade well for a profitable return cargo. If the vessel traded for pepper in Sumatra or coffee at Mocha or cloves at Zanzibar or tea at Canton, the Captain must not only see to it he acquired what could be sold at a profit in Salem or Boston, but he must be ever watchful for pilfering by natives or an armed attack in force aimed at taking his ship. These Captains, usually men under thirty, were given everything to work with by their owners; a fine ship, a good Yankee crew, enough cannon to deliver a healthy broadside at any pirate, kegs of silver coin for purchases and so much discretion that they were rulers for the duration of the voyage. They were gone a year and an outward or homeward passage of 110 days was considered excellent. Of a very well regarded young lady, it was often said, "She deserves an East India Captain."

EAST WIND

The salvation of Bostonians on a sweltering summer day. In a heat wave office workers have one eye on the weather vane and if it flips over to East, everyone looks happy, for they know that in a few minutes they will get the smell of roasting coffee from warehouses on the harborfront and the tang of salt water from the Bay. The atmosphere changes, everyone feels brisker, more work gets done and if it is a good breeze, men put on their coats and the girls get up to shut windows. While all of the coastal cities have the relief of the east wind in torrid spells, the Bostonians in their hot downtown office buildings appreciate it the most. Sometimes it is a strong and persistent breeze felt as far inland as Concord; more often a gentle turn of the wind bringing relief no further than the weather side of Beacon Hill. The east wind is an institution so famous that the Boston & Maine named one of its best locomotives for it. Like many good things, it is fleeting and temporary and is soon gone; only the northwest wind brings lasting relief from a heat wave. People from other parts of the country have the notion that in Boston the east wind blows only in summer. That is quite erroneous; we have it in the other seasons, but then we say it is "raw" or "biting" or "disagreeable."

EATING TOBACCO

Another name for a plug of chewing tobacco. Today the ash tray has replaced the spitoon in our New England scene and few of us realize how common chewing formerly was. No public place was without a facility to receive the expectorations of those who enjoyed this use of tobacco. Even in the Superior Court fresh boxes of white pine sawdust were placed within the bar enclosure every morning for the accommodation of the lawyers. After a day of trying a difficult case to a jury the hard pressed brethren of the bar would have turned the white sawdust to a dark mahogany brown. In those days accuracy of expectoration was a valued male accomplishment; many an informal contest for modest stakes took place down at the village store and at clambakes or the local fair or at the station while waiting for the

Boston train. Had not this art passed into oblivion we would doubtless be viewing such competitions on television. Varieties of spitoons were numerous, dark crockery, white or tinted china with all sorts of designs and, grandest of all, brass. No well run hotel or club or barber shop was without its tall brass spitoon, freshly shined every morning, a receptacle lending dignity and class, engraved with the name of the establishment and giving forth a metallic ring whenever a good marksman made a bullseye.

EGG MONEY

On the old time farm, where a small flock of hens was a sideline, it was customary for the wife to have the money from the sale of the eggs not required for family use. Even in towns, hens were common, for the backyards were large with plenty of room for a coop, and the scraps from the table went a long way toward feeding them. In those hard scrabble days this source of funds, carefully used, enabled the housewife to make very occasional purchases of store clothes, a tablecloth, a fancy vase, or even a nice soapstone sink for her kitchen. One who wished to speak ill of any man might say, "He is mean enough to take his wife's egg money."

EPIZOOTIC

A variety of influenza afflicting horses, sometimes reaching epidemic proportions. The epizootic was rampant in Boston in November 1872 and most of the fire horses lay ill in their stalls, completely incapable of any work. When the fateful Box 52 hit on the city's fire alarm tapper for the blazing warehouse at Kingston and Summer Streets, the engines had to be hauled to the scene by hand. Two score men are none too many to move a steam fire engine weighing several tons, even over streets with but gentle grades. So the department was very late in arriving, the big building erupted flame from cellar to roof, nearby structures had begun to burn, and the first alarm response was fewer than the normal number of engines, because the authorities had reduced the running card on account of the epizootic. The apparatus summoned by the second and third and later alarms took even longer, the fire was out of hand when they got there and the conflagration roared through downtown Boston to the harbor's edge. The epizootic disease of horses bears much of the responsibility for the disaster; and more justly than the infamy attached to the immortal cow of Mrs. O'Leary of Chicago, for this epidemic was one of the prime reasons that an ordinary fire got wholly out of control and leveled an important part of Boston.

EVERYTHING'S DRAWING

A Yankee mariner's reply to the common question "How are you," if it so happens life is using him well just now. The expression originally referred to a ship with all sail set and a following breeze filling all

55

of her canvas. It came to be used not only as to a ship for which all was going well, but for a man who was functioning to the very best of his capabilities. But a true Yankee will reserve this answer for a friend he judges really wishes to know how the world is using him. As for those who say "How are you" without sincerity and for want of something intelligent to say, he does not venture to commit himself.

EYES

Like two burned holes in a blanket. This is the description of one who is indeed poorly, his face pale and drawn so his eyes stand out prominently in a wane countenance. Illness, over-fatigue or a wild night are generally the cause of this state. Some imaginative fellow, seeking to vary the old and familiar expression, said of some badly run-down person: "His eyes look like two boiled onions in a cellar wall."

FIRE BALLOON

An ingenious device used in an earlier day to help celebrate the Glorious Fourth. Made of paper, it had excelsior or a sponge in the lower part upon which the celebrant poured a little alcohol or kerosene. When he touched a match to it the resulting fire caused hot air to fill the bag of the balloon, the hot air made it rise, it burned brightly in the night sky, trailed a pretty shower of sparks and then it came apart and dropped to earth. Upon these occasions when it dropped not to earth, but upon some citizen's dry wooden shingle roof, there was added to the fourth of July celebration an extra feature. The box was pulled, the fire alarm whistle blew, everyone gathered to watch, the apparatus came galloping in and if their arrival was timely, a chemical line sufficed to extinguish the blazing shingles. If the firemen were elsewhere when the alarm sounded and there was a delayed response, the victim often lost the roof and attic rooms, and had the rest of the house well soaked by the big water lines. Fire balloons, prohibited by statute, are now extinct, along with such other patriotic manifestations as cannon crackers, dynamite caps on street car rails and touching off backhouses.

FIRE TRUMPET

A large brass speaking trumpet used by officers of the "hand-tub" fire engines of the 19th century. Theoretically their purpose was to amplify orders shouted to their men in the din and uproar at the scene of the fire. As often they were used to beat time on some part of the hand operated fire engine as the officer stood on top, urging his two score men to greater efforts at the two long parallel "brakes," or pump handles. In those days hydrants were few and the engines usually drew their water from cisterns and wells at a distance, which required that one pump into another, thus "relaying" the water to the fire. The hose of the first engine led into an opening at the top of a water chamber on the second in line and if the men of the first could out-pump the crew of the second, the water rose, overflowed, wet number two's feet and they were "washed." This was a disgrace and they would be twitted about it around town for months afterward. Many a fire trumpet was banged into a piece of crumpled brass by an officer frantically urging his men to greater efforts, lest they be "washed," or trying to get the extra ounce of effort to "wash" the engine company up ahead. So much did the trumpet come to be a symbol of command that today it appears on the collar ornaments of the officers. Why any real fireman ever needed anything to amplify his voice has never been satisfactorily explained.

FIREMAN'S MUSTER

A day when every club that owns an old fashioned hand operated fire engine (hand tub) meets in some park or field to see who can throw a stream of water the farthest. They come from 50 miles around; their fire engines, glistening with scarlet and gilt paint and shining brass work, are mounted on motor trucks for the long trip. In the morning the old hand tubs, drawn by their men, are paraded, along with bands of music, drum and bugle corps, interesting old motor engines and perhaps a steamer with three white horses and a fire under her boiler. After the parade comes a whopping big feed. Then in the afternoon the hand tubs, often twenty or more, have their trial of strength, the crews pump mightily, there is a great clanking noise and a stream equal to anything modern apparatus can do shoots out toward the long paper used to measure the distance the water is thrown. Judges jot down the figures in their notebooks. Work on the "brakes" of a hand tub in competition is a man killing job and the crews pump at top speed for not much more than a minute and they can put a stream more than 250 feet. At fires in the old days they pumped at a slower pace and there always was a relief crew standing by to "spell' them at the brakes. Hand tubs have names like TORRENT, PROTECTION, CATARACT, EAGLE or VOLUNTEER with occasionally one more picturesque, like SILVER GRAY, ANDROSCOGGIN and Marblehead's famous OKOMAKAMESIT.

FISH, CUT BAIT OR GO ASHORE

Along the Yankee coast this means "make up your mind; do one thing or the other or get out of here." Aboard a fishing vessel, be it a two masted schooner on the Grand Banks or a dory working the off-shore ledges, idle hands are not tolerated. A man must either wet a line, apply himself to cutting up the noisome carrion used for bait, or he will be set ashore forthwith by his skipper.

FISH PEDLAR

With his little horse and light wagon he used to drive slowly through the streets of our coastal towns, occasionally blowing on a long tin fish horn that gave forth as unmusical a note as ever assailed the human ear. "Fresh fish," he shouted, and he meant fresh fish, for what he had in the wagon was the morning's catch, packed in wet seaweed and ice. Housewives heard the braying, metallic blat of his horn while he was yet afar and they were at the gate to see if he had any halibut and if not, codfish or flounder would do. Pawing around in the seaweed in the back of his wagon, the pedlar would bring forth one fish after another until he found what his customer liked. Then he laid the fish on a board and with a long knife, razor keen, cut off head, tail and fins and tossed them to a half dozen hungry cats who had been trailing him since he rounded the corner. While they fought over this gurry, he weighed the fish, pocketed his money and drove off. Always mindful of his reputation, he was particular not to offer for sale a fish that had been ashore for more than one day. It is only since the advent of modern refrigeration that any but salt fish have been available in communities at a distance from the seashore.

FLOOD CONTROL DAM

This structure is of any size, built at the end of a valley or gulch in hill country and with an aperture not a great deal larger than the brook or small river which carries off the normal rainfall. In ordinary weather the land behind the dam, perhaps reaching a mile or more upstream, is used for pasture or raising crops. If there is a flood due to the sudden melting of winter's snow or a deluge of rain that runs quickly off the steep hills, the dam permits three or four times the normal flow of the stream to run through the aperture, but any greater amount of water is held back. Thus a reservoir is formed and impounded in the valley during the period of greatest flood danger, draining gradually through the hole over a period of days and perhaps weeks. This is a single purpose dam for flood control only, having the advantage of allowing the use of the valley land for agricultural purposes under all but the most unusual conditions. Although a dam creating a permanent reservoir provides a source of hydro electric power as well as controlling floods; it destroys the agricultural usefulness of a large area of fertile valley land. The danger of such economic losses has resulted in many controversies over dams designed for both flood control and electric power. At East Barre, Vermont, a typical flood control dam, while controlling one of the headwaters of the dangerous Winooski River in times of high water, permits agriculture use of the valley land in normal times. The importance of this lies in the fact that Vermont without its valley farms would be a depressed area indeed.

FOOT STOVE

A small square box-like affair made of tin, with small holes punched in sides and top. In the days when fireplaces were the only means of heating a building, the old settlers would fill their foot stoves with glowing coals, take them to church when they went to Sunday meetings and put them on the floor to keep their feet warm. The Meeting House had no central heating equipment of any sort, the sermons were long and the winters severe, so anyone who forgot his foot stove stood a good chance of finding his feet so chilled he would have trouble leaving the premises when the minister had at last concluded his remarks. The religious services of some of the sects more lately come to New England include enough standing and kneeling to maintain a fair degree of circulation in the body even in an unheated church. The Puritan did not have the benefit of this more active ritual; he was obliged to sit and listen, and the red hot flames of hell the minister put in his sermon were not half as much use on a mid-January Sunday morning as a good foot stove well packed with glowing coals from a stout oak log.

FOREIGNER

Term applied by Marbleheaders to those not native to the place, regardless of race, creed, color or previous condition of servitude. One born in Marblehead might qualify as a native, but to be sure of that status he must be able to prove that not only his parents, but his grandparents first saw the light of the day in the town. It is said that a candidate for Selectman was defeated at the polls when it was called to the attention of the voters by his oppo nents that he was born in the Salem Hospital, and was therefore a foreigner. Sometimes the expression "a blow in" is used to refer to a foreigner very recently arrived; that is, someone who has not been around more than ten or fifteen years. This attitude is found in some degree in many New England towns.

FRESH BOILED OWL

By most careful research philologists have learned that many years ago, in colonial times, a Yankee whose provisions had run short in the dead of winter, took his gun and set forth through the snows in search of game to feed his family. His luck was poor, he sighted nothing until near sundown, when he spied a big owl perched on the limb of a blasted pine. He let fly with his gun, got the critter and lugged it home to feed his wife and hungry children. She boiled it and when it came out of the kettle is closely resembled old Uncle Jehosophat when he was in his cups, which was most of the time. From then on, whenever he saw Uncle Jehosophat under the weather, he said he was "as stewed as a fresh boiled owl." The term spread and became common and has endured to this day, an instance of how something that one man said so long ago can become a part of the language. This phenomenon continues to puzzle philologists, although research upon it continues and we may be on the threshold of an important breakthrough in this field of science.

GAM

When two whaling ships met at sea,
they backed their foretopsails, hove to
and the crews visited back and forth and
had a GAM, which meant they swapped
news, told yarns, exchanged books, traded
sharply for various articles they had bought in some
port or made during the watch below. Sailors were
great readers, so they welcomed the opportunity to
get new books. They loved to make small objects,
particularly scrimshaw carvings of whale ivory and
they liked to enlarge their collections with examples
of the other fellow's work. But most of all they
craved news. What whaling conditions were in other
parts of the broad Pacific, which ports were friendly
and which were not, word of friends on other ships
that had been met, was information more precious
than gold. More than anything, they wished to know
what was happening at home. Aboard a vessel at sea
two years or more, a sailor might learn in a GAM
with a ship more recently departed, that he was the
father of twins or that one of his folks with "rooma-
tiz" was feeling a lot better, or perhaps that one of
the kindred had fared forth on the last voyage, now
resting in peace in his long home beneath the elms in
the graveyard. There might even be a letter put
aboard one ship on the chance it might meet the vessel the addressee was serving on. When everyone was
talked out, the two vessels braced their yards to the
wind to go on with their long search for whales.

GAS MANTLE

A small cotton mesh in size and shape like a very wide and short thumb. This device was soaked in thorium and cerium nitrate at the factory and came to the ultimate consumer in a little cardboard box marked "fragile." The householder affixed it to one of the jets of his gas light, touched a match to it, and the cotton burned in a quick flame leaving the ash in the same size and shape and mesh texture. Then he turned on the gas, lighted it and the mantle became incandescent, giving a greenish white light much stronger than an ordinary "fishtail" gas flame. This little mantle served well until a sudden jar or a clumsy movement broke it. Invented by Welsbach, the gas mantle was the step in the evolution of lighting between the simple gas flame and the improved electric bulb. It was a much better light than the first dim electric incandescent lamps, but the steady improvement in the art of electricity finally made the mantle obsolete. Today it is used only on portable gasoline lanterns for campers, and similar equipment. Few now realize that gas was originally used almost entirely for lighting, it being the stage following the kerosene lamps on the living room table and in brackets in the kitchen. Gas heating followed the gas light, its development proceeding from a single burner cooking flat for one doing light housekeeping in a third floor room to the modern all purpose cook stove and the furnace that serves an entire house.

GERRYMANDER

To divide into election districts in a way designed
to give a political party an advantage. In 1812, when
Elbridge Gerry was Governor of Massachusetts, such
a senatorial district was created that began at Salis-
bury and included Amesbury, Haverhill, Methuen,
Andover, Middleton, Danvers, Lynnfield, Salem, Mar-

blehead, Lynn and Chelsea. A diagram of this monstrosity hung on the wall of the Federalist newspaper CENTINEL and the famous painter, Gilbert Stuart, visiting the editor, picked up a crayon, added head, wings and claws to this long, thin, district shaped like some reptile, and announced that it was a salamander. The editor, who had no use for Republican Governor Gerry, said, "A Gerrymander, you mean." This political creature is living today.

GLASSIE

A large "marble" made of glass and having in its transparent interior beautiful spirals of red and green and blue porcelain, or, in a very choice one, a silver rabbit or a golden rooster. The boy who owns the glassie put it on the ground and allows other boys to pop at it with ordinary marbles from a distance which he decides. He picks up the marbles that miss. If one hits his glassie, title passes, and the successful marksman takes possession of the prize. He may decide he likes it and put it on the mantlepiece at home, or his thirst for more marbles may be so strong that he immediately puts it on the ground to be popped at. For anyone who asks what good marbles are, it might be explained that they are approximately equivalent in value to horse chestnuts.

GOING DOWN TO SALT WATER

The expression inland folks used when they made up their minds to hitch up old Dobbin, put the chil-

dren in back and the picnic basket under the seat and start out for a day at the beach. The children went in wading, collected round stones, starfish, great quantities of seaweed, and, if not carefully watched, they might try to take a jellyfish into custody. While Ma collected specimens of the more delicate marine growths to press between the leaves of a book when she got home, Pa, if he was a real vigorous fellow, might go for a swim. Then, over a driftwood fire, they cooked dinner; generally something they brought with them, but perhaps Ma had bought a couple of quarts of clams and attempted a chowder. She was a smart one if she succeeded, for inland folks don't understand such things and to make a good chowder, one must have been brought up within the sound of the pounding surf. In the gloaming of the summer day they would jog home with their beach stones and periwinkles and odd bits of driftwood, the kids fussing about their sunburned legs and wanting to know when they could have supper.

GORE

A term used to describe a tract of land long, narrow, irregular and roughly triangular in outline, somewhat resembling in shape the horn of a beef critter. This expression, once common in Northern New England, refers to odd pieces of land left over when old time surveyors, no believers in wasting time, got done running the lines on a good farm or a promising piece of timber. In those days land was plentiful and labor was not, so a buyer was interested only in the workable area and was content to leave poor pieces of hill or ledge or swamp for the seller, his heirs and the town tax collector to worry about. This was quite agreeable to the surveyors, who had no wish to wade through bogs, climb cliffs, or tramp through bramble patches measuring out land that was no good anyway. This procedure resembled the technique of a boy cutting himself a piece of fruit cake, making sure to get the nuts and the citron. A gore of land is sometimes found between two towns or even two counties, in instances where the authorities of both planned to leave the other fellow with some worthless terrain or where the surveyors were in poor condition the day they were out there.

GRAB

The New Englander is not and never has been the grasping and hard fisted fellow others have made him out to be. In any transaction he wants the other man to get something worthwhile out of the deal. His business philosophy is summed up in a Yankee maxim the first part of which is "Never grab with both hands." Yet he does not propose to let anyone trade him out of his trousers and send him home with a barrel around his middle. Hence the second part of his maxim is "Just grab with one." With this as a guide he continues to do middling well in a land lacking almost any natural advantages other than its always varied beauty and the fact that he lives and works there.

GRASSHOPPER

The weather vane on the cupola of Faneuil Hall that has told Bostonians where the wind is since 1742, the year wealthy merchant, Peter Faneuil, gave the building to the town for a public market. An enormous example of the grasshopper species, made of copper and fashioned by the skillful hands of Shem Drowne along the lines of a similar insect on the Royal Exchange in London, it has maintained its perch high above the "Cradle of Liberty" most of the time since the building was dedicated. In the 1755 earthquake it fetched up in the street and lost a leg, it went through a fire and several reconstructions of the Hall, but with the help of clever coppersmiths the grasshopper has remained in good health to this day. Everyone is expected to know what critter heads to windward atop Faneuil Hall. He who comes up with an incorrect answer is certainly not a Bostonian, but someone from the outer fringes of civilization.

GREASY LUCK

The New Bedford and Nantucket version of "Good luck." Whaling was the principal business of these two ports, and whales were valuable for the oil tried out from the blubber in a brick furnace on deck. If the ship was lucky, it caught whales, got them alongside, cut off the great chunks of blubber, hoisted them on deck and tried out the oil. The decks were so greasy while this was going on that any sailor not extremely careful might slip, fall and rap his head on the hard planking. This dangerous and malodorous condition of the deck bothered the sailors not at all, for the faster the whales came, the sooner would the oil barrels be filled and the ship homeward bound. So it came to be that "greasy luck" was "good luck." Some vessels that had the reverse of greasy luck, searched the oceans of the world (usually the North Pacific) for as long as three years before they at last had all their barrels full and the ship headed for home.

GROUNDED OUT

To people in the small ports along the Yankee coast, this is not a baseball expression, but a term

71

describing the position of a small vessel alongside a wharf when the tide goes out. The further down east one goes, the greater the rise and fall of the tide, with the result that a pier that has plenty of depth at high water may have only mud when the tide is out. A lumber schooner or fisherman or packet boat that calls at these small ports and "landings" must expect to spend part of her time resting on the harbor bottom, "grounded out." Therefore, such a vessel must not be built on lines too sharp, for if she does not have a bottom somewhat flat, she will tip over or "careen" when she grounds out at low water and something is bound to give.

GROUNDHOG

The woodchuck, a chunky little animal well known to farmers and suburbanites with vegetable gardens, for in one night he can strip the leaves off a couple of rows of string beans, leaving only the sad looking stems. He is very intelligent; as winter approaches he takes to his burrow deep in the earth and goes to sleep in his little bed of sweet grass and clover, thus avoiding the mean weather without putting himself to all the trouble the birds and wealthy human beings go to in traveling thousands of miles south to be away from snow and ice. February 2nd is Groundhog Day, named for him because then he pokes his head from the entrance of his burrow, which is always under a huge boulder or the root of a big tree, and looks around to see what the weather is. He ventures forth and if he can see his shadow, there is to be six weeks more of winter, but if it is overcast and he sees no shadow, then there is to be an early Spring. So goes the legend, but old Captain Lamson of Ipswich says the woodchuck comes out February 2nd because after sleeping two months his bedroom gets mighty close and needs an airing, and since it hasn't any windows, he opens the door. This business about seeing his shadow is bosh, says the Captain. February 2nd is also known as Candlemas Day, an occasion of religious significance in some churches.

GUNDALOW

More of a scow than a ship, this wide, shallow draft vessel has been used along the Yankee coast since earliest colonial times to transport heavy or bulky freight such as hay, lumber, brick, firewood and coal. Its freeboard is low, so it is no sea boat and a skipper with any sense would hesitate to take it out of sight of land. Most useful in a tidal creek or salt river, it did the heavy work in days when roads were few and so poor as to be usable only in good weather. Its square or lateen sail was some help in short trips up and down the estuaries, and the crews had oars and poles to help it along. However, most of the work in getting this clumsy craft from here to there was done by the tide; it departed from some upstream pier or landing on the ebb tide

73

and rode downstream to the seaport always to be found at the mouth of a river. Returning, it always waited for the flood tide. In these salt rivers navigational hazards such as tide rips and treacherous rocks were frequent and the crew observed the genial custom of having a stout peg of rum once the gundalow was past a particularly dangerous spot. Railroads, trucks and modern hard surfaced roads have made these slow, lumbering craft largely obsolete today.

HALFWAY ROCK

 A bare, rugged rock formation well out to sea from Salem Bay and midway between Boston Light and Cape Ann. Inhabited only by gulls and shag and ringed with foaming breakers in rough weather, it has a silhouette that on a misty day has made many a yachtsman think for a moment that a heavy cruiser was inward bound. In the old days the Marblehead fishermen, commencing a voyage to the Grand Banks, used to heave to and throw pennies onto the rock for good luck, an offering upon the altar of some vaguely understood salt water deity. A thrifty Marbleheader of long ago went ashore with a couple of buckets and filled them with the pennies thrown there by outbound mariners. He gained nothing, for his profits were consumed in repairs to his person after his fellow townsmen, learning of his sacrilege, visited vengeance upon him.

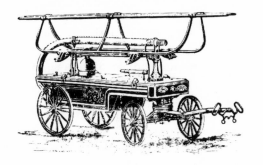

HAND TUB

A hand operated fire engine. Originating with a
crude machine first used in the 17th Century it had
become by 1850 a first class piece of apparatus capable of taking suction from a well, cistern or brook,
pumping through a long line of hose and delivering
a strong stream at the scene of the fire. Its great
weakness was its hand power. Two dozen men were
required to work the long pump handles (brakes) and
another two dozen had to be at hand to relieve them
when they tired. A large fraction of the able bodied
men in any city or town were needed for the fire department, always on call to answer an alarm rung
upon the church bells. Rivalries between engine companies grew up, resulting sometimes in fights at the
scene of the fire that received much more attention
than extinguishing the blaze. Therefore when the
steam fire engine was perfected in the mid 19th

century, it was a great relief to the municipal authorities to accomplish with an engineer and a stoker what had previously required three score truculent and undisciplined citizens. But the hand tubs were great fun. Everyone had a fireman's helmet, ran with the old machine, and was proud of it. They spoke ill of the other fire companies at all times, enjoyed their clambakes and chowders, marched in parades, shined their engines and returned home from fires exhausted and gloriously dirty. Many of the hand tubs have been preserved and every summer firemen's musters are held with a dozen companies competing to see who can throw the longest stream and make the most noise. For a while they punch out as fine a stream as the most modern motor fire engine but after a quarter hour they shut down, the judges measure the distance and the men report at the supply truck for a ham sandwich and a bottle of beer.

HAPPY AS A CLAM AT HIGH TIDE

The way folks along the Yankee Coast describe a state of contentment, plenitude and security. For a clam, high tide is his time for maximum felicity. He is in his native element, a situation pleasing to every mortal being. The sea which nourishes him covers his lodging place to a depth of at least eight feet, so he need take no thought of how he is to be fed. And he is secure, for not until the tide is low and the long expanse of beach or mud flats glistens wetly in the sun, is the presence of his home beneath the surface betrayed to a man with a clam rake or a predatory animal or bird. Implicit in this expression is the thought that the clam's happiness, like that of all the rest of us, is but temporary.

HARNESS BULL

One driven in harness to the place where his prime function was to be performed, usually ahead of a buggy or democrat wagon. Rarely occurring was the combination of a farmer with the skill and tact to train a bull to the harness and a bull sufficiently tractable to accept such restraint. When a man managed to perfect such an arrangement he had a very profitable thing indeed, for he could save the owner of a cow the time consuming task of leading her perhaps miles to her tryst. A farmer who left his cow in the barnyard to chew her cud and await the arrival of the harness bull could attend to his haying or his corn, and he was well ahead of the game if he paid a double fee. The owner of the bull had an easy time of it driving about the countryside in his buggy, unharnessing his critter and leaning on the fence until the fee was earned, although he had to be careful not to accept too much business, for bulls, too, get tired. "Harness bull" is used in a wholly different connection by the underworld to designate a uniformed police officer, thus differentiating him from a plain clothes man.

HEATER PIECE

The corner made by two streets or roads that intersect at an acute angle, so called because its outline resembles that of a flatiron. Farmers sometimes call a field of that shape "the heater piece." The famous Flatiron Building in New York was so named by reason of a similar fancy.

HELL ROOM

When one holds a fellow mortal in very low esteem, the opinion is frequently expressed by the statement, "I wouldn't give him hell room." No one has ever offered to explain what lower apartment might be made available.

HELL TO PAY AND NO PITCH HOT

In any critical situation, large or small, these words come naturally. Sometimes it is "the devil to pay and no pitch hot," the word "pay" here not meaning to hand over money or something else of value but to apply pitch to the seams of a vessel. Careful lexicographers, after the most painstaking research, have concluded that "the devil" is one of the lower strakes or planks of a boat, and the metaphor intends to suggest a workman facing the task of "paying" the seam to make it watertight, only to find his kettle of pitch is stone cold and he can do nothing. When the expression is "hell to pay" one visualizes hell as a ship, the lower strakes of which some unhappy workman must "pay," and with no fire under his pitch kettle his predicament is one of the classic examples of frustration.

HILL OF BEANS

Another one of the "it don't amount to" expressions. (See Hannah Cook). Apparently a Yankee feels that a hill of beans is considerably less valuable than a hill of corn or a hill of potatoes, or perhaps he never put in any time considering the matter, and says "it don't amount to a hill of beans" for no better reason than that it rolls off his tongue more easily.

HOLDING GROUND

A mariner's term descriptive of an area of the sea off the coast where the flukes of an anchor would catch in mud or sand or on angular rocks and hold. Charts of a coast line were marked here and there with the legend "holding ground" to show places where a ship, when the wind was on shore, might let go her anchors and hold her position no matter how stiff a breeze might blow. Few things

79

were more important to a ship master than to know the location of good holding ground along any coast he sailed. Lacking a firm hold for his anchors on a bottom of hard clay or smooth rock, his vessel was "dragging anchor." Helplessly he watched as the lee shore became nearer. Then, unless luck was with him and the anchor flukes caught on something, his ship fetched up in the pounding surf. On some of the coasts where Yankee ships traded, the survivors had to look sharp lest they ended up as the piece de resistance in cannibal feasts. If they were clever, they lived on coconuts and turtle's eggs until another ship sighted them or they managed to build a raft and escape. So in common Yankee speech, a man who said he was looking for "good holding ground" meant a position in which he could stay while conditions were adverse.

HOLD THE THOUGHT

To remember something, more particularly to make a mental note of something which cannot now be discussed because of present exigencies, but which may be developed later by discussion or reflection. So the suggestion "hold the thought" means "file it for future reference and be sure not to lose it."

HOOK AND LADDER

Hauled by a crew of men on two long drag ropes and much lighter than today's truck with its long aerial, it did the same type of work at the fire. If householders were leaning from the windows of a burning building, the ladder men rescued them. When a hose line was to be taken to an upper floor, they placed a ladder; and they had axes to dig out a smouldering fire. Today we call it the "ladder truck," leaving off the word "hook," because that describes an operation no longer a part of fire fighting. The old timers had the notion that if they tore a house apart, the fire could be more easily extinguished. Holes were chopped in the top of the wall, the big hooks were inserted, ropes running from each to the ground were taken by a gang of men, and they heaved until the side of the house came off. Then the hosemen directed their streams into the blazing interior. Experience showed that as much was accomplished by streams directed through the windows with less effort and less damage to the building, so the old time "hook" is now a museum piece. Today's ladder truck carries the "plaster hook," a cutting tool on a long handle to make holes in walls and ceilings so a stream may be directed into a concealed fire. Not to be confused with the old fashioned hook used for tearing off part of a building.

HORSE CHESTNUT

One of the most useless fruits of Mother Earth, a thoughtless fellow might say. Such a person must, however, be unaware that a horse chestnut carried in one's pocket infallibly wards off rheumatism. Furthermore, there never lived a boy not familiar with the nut. In autumn every tree is watched by dozens of urchins, waiting for the burrs to drop. The morning after a sharp frost is the time to find them in the dry leaves at the roadside. But impatient, boys usually hurry things by throwing sticks and stones into the tree, bring down leaves and branches with the burrs and occasionally scoring on a light of glass in a nearby house. Then an angry home owner bursts from the door and there is the added fun of a chase, which the boys always win because they go through a hole in a hedge or over a fence with an agility no adult can match. In accordance with the ancient doctrine of "chips," the boys may later arrange to compensate the man for his square of glass, the money usually being paid over by the father of one of them. This expense they do not regret; it is little to pay for the pleasure of hearing the tinkle of a broken window and the excitement of a good chase. Ask any boy what he is going to do with the horse chestnuts he acquires by so much time and effort and he talks vaguely of making a pipe or carving faces. Although he might get around to some such enterprise, what he really wants is merely the pleasure of possessing these glistening brown objects with their fresh white tops. In the fall his pockets bulge with them, his desk is lined with them and mother probably will find a sizeable box of them under his bed. And if she is wise she does not disturb his carefully stored treasure.

HORSE CLOG

A round piece of good oak or hickory slightly wider than the horse's hoof with fastenings on the top so it could be secured to the animals foot. Well shod with four of these, the horse was ready to clump up and down a salt marsh or inland meadow in haying time without sinking into the wet, spongy soil. A farmer who had marsh or meadow land always owned horse clogs and a hay rick with extra broad tires so it would not get mired in the soft going. The hay from an inland meadow was thin, mixed with reeds, purple flag and pitcher plants, yet it was good feed for cows in the winter, when they had to stay in the barn or in the yard and needed a ration that kept them busy. The hay from marshes along tidal creeks had some nutriment, yielded the taste of salt all animals crave and was widely used to bed down horses. The farmer near the shore often stored his salt hay out on the marsh in cocks set on a circle of stakes called "staddles," where it was well above an unusually high tide, until he put the clogs on his horse, hitched up to the broad tired wagon and went after it. Or he might load it onto a shallow bottomed gundalow floated up the creek a high tide, then sail his craft to town and sell his salt hay to the stable owners.

HORSE HAT

In the days when the "be kind to animals" movement was really gaining momentum, in the latter part of the last century, it came to be felt that a horse should not be expected to endure the blazing summer sun without a straw hat any more than should a human being. Clever designers, probably with background of Parisian training, developed a horse hat of tasteful proportions with holes through which the animal's ears protruded. Although no ribbon came with the hat, some owners with artistic perceptions added one and perhaps flowers from a neighbor's garden, thus giving their horse a debonair summertime appearance. Horses were protected against the fierce heat of summer, yet the custom of providing horses with straw hats died out, possibly because no way was ever found of discovering whether the animals appreciated the thoughtfulness of their owners.

HOSE REEL

In the old time fire department a light carriage carrying hose wound around a big cylindrical reel, its mission being to connect to the outlet on the hand engine and lay a line to the fire. The hose company did not have the heavy work of pumping, nor was it involved in the fierce competitions that the hand tub men so dearly loved. They were gaily painted little vehicles often hauled to the fire by boys. Of course they did race each other to fires, occasional collisions resulted; sometimes they tipped over taking a corner at speed. The old time hose was leather, more difficult to handle than what we have today.

Hence, a reel was necessary, whereas the modern hose, more flexible, may be tightly packed into the much more compact and convenient hose body in the rear part of the motor pumper.

HUB

This word means Boston, of course. Everyone knows that all roads lead to Boston, as the spokes lead to the hub of a wheel. All railroads lead to the city, too. One catches the Boston train in Malden or in Ipswich or Pawtucket or Nashua or at Dudley Street. A Boston train departs from Washington, D. C., making New York as a way station; a Boston train leaves Halifax and Albany and Montreal and

Intervale. Only in far away places, where civilization is in a formative stage, is a Boston train lacking. Boston is, of course, the center of commerce, culture and learning. That this is not merely a national matter was best stated by Dr. Oliver Wendell Holmes in his "Autocrat of the Breakfast Table" when he observed that Boston is "the hub of the universe." The exact center of the Hub of the Universe is the dome of the State House.

HUCKLEBERRY GRUNT

An old fashioned Cape Cod dessert. First pick 4 cups of huckleberries, put them in a saucepan on top of the stove to stew, add 1 or 1½ cups sugar, more or less according to taste, then a pinch of salt for good luck. When berries are done, drop small dumplings, made with an egg, into the sauce to steam fifteen minutes with the lid on securely. When you lift the lid you will find the dumplings fluffed up prettily. Put them on plates, pour the sauce over them, serve hot and see what the men folks say. This dish may be made with blueberries or wild blackberries, if these are what you find in the far pasture when you go out with your pail. The origin of this euphonious name is as yet unascertained by the philologists, although some hold it to be descriptive of the satisfied guttural uttered by a hungry man who has eaten well. If a dissatisfied man may be said to be disgruntled, then certainly a satisfied man is gruntled.

HUSHER

This was the finely worked crochet piece our ancestors fitted over the cover of an earthernware chamber pot so that cloth was interposed between the under side of the cover and the rim. While the vessel was a necessity and the cover highly desirable, a housekeeper possessed of the finer perceptions tried to eliminate the clang of crockery upon crockery that resounded through the house in the still watches of the night when some sleepy user was clumsy in the use of the convenience under the bed. Hence the husher, an article of utility and ornament upon which many a lady of a bygone day lavished hours of careful needlework. Unfortunately specimens are hard to find in our museums.

ICE HOUSE

 Farmers always had ice houses, little structures often built into a side hill, where they stored chunks cut from the pond in the dead of winter. Buried in sawdust the ice lasted through the summer. In the 19th century the technique of commercial ice harvesting developed rapidly; great ice houses were built at ponds near the cities and in mid-winter, after a couple of good zero spells, the crews went to work. Horses drew the "groovers" that cut the ice into blocks, men with poles pushed the cakes along an open channel toward an incline leading up to the ice house, steel claws were hooked onto each piece and a rope led over a pulley and down to a horse. Up went each cake by horse power, to be slid into place by men working inside. Sometimes the hoisting was done by a steam donkey engine. When the ice house was full, a thick layer of marsh hay was spread on top, and this, together with double walls packed with sawdust or tanbark, insulated the ice so that it lasted through the hottest summer weather with little shrinkage. Sometimes in the work out on the pond a horse fell into the water. This was foreseen and therefore each animal had a "choke rope" around his neck. One man held this while another slipped a rope around the tail and passed the end to someone else, who quickly fastened it to the whiffle tree of another horse. A word, and out came the victim to land safe on the ice. To supply Boston some companies built enormous ice houses in New Hampshire so they would not be left without a crop by a mild Massachusetts winter. From the big establishment North of Franklin and at Milton several freight cars loaded with ice would be dispatched for Boston every summer day. Mechanical refrigeration is here, the art of ice harvesting is vanished and the huge ice houses have burned or have been torn down. The ice man who came to the back door with a heavy cake on his back is on his way to join other legendary American figures like the tin peddler and the stage coach driver.

INDIAN SUMMER

A spell of real fine weather in October or November. On such days there is little wind, smoke rises in a straight column, the sun is warm and the sky is blue, except for a haze on the horizon, and the air is caressing. Folks love to burn dry leaves and the smell is in the atmosphere everywhere. An Indian summer day is a great time to play hookey; boys are missing from their seats in class and men sneak away from the office to get in just one more round of golf. If such weather comes on a weekend, everybody who has a vehicle with four good wheels has it rolling, the roads are crowded with motorists out to see the autumn foliage in all its glory of scarlet and russet and gold, and they come home in the gloaming, making traffic jams at every important intersection. Indian summer comes after we have had our first rugged weather; the line storm or a couple of killing frosts. It is fine weather the more appreciated for that it is so soon to be taken away; an interlude, a respite before the grim vise of Winter really grips us.

INSIDE PLUMBING

An expression used by those who lived in a less mechanized age in referring to a flush toilet installed in a dwelling house. This then radical advance was thus differentiated from what was universally used prior to the time American inventive genius provided the people with a contraption that accomplished so much with one pull of a chain. A lady whose parsimonious husband made her continue to use a backhouse in the yard once petulantly said, "If I die and you get married again and give your second wife inside plumbing, I'll come back to haunt you."

IPSWICH RIVER

A beautiful stream rising in North Reading, in Middlesex County, and then passing into Essex County and flowing through Middleton, Danvers and Topsfield, finally reaching the ocean at Ipswich. All the way it winds through a lovely country of woodland, farm and meadow. Anglers live for the opening of the season so they can range along its banks again fishing for trout and pickerel. One man who had fished the stream since he was a lad, left orders that his body be cremated and his ashes strewn upon the waters of the Ipswich. "Nowhere that I know," he wrote "is there on this earth so near an approach to Heaven, and it is there, where I have spent so many happy hours, that I wish my mortal remains to be." His time did not come until he was an old man and then his wishes were carried out to the letter. The service for the committal of the dead was held on a wooden bridge over the river and his ashes floated downstream through the country he had loved so well.

IRON DOG

A noble hound or coach dog, a triumph of the iron monger's art, which adorned the lawn of a prosperous man in the latter part of the 19th century. Generally the iron dog had taken his stance on premises where stood a three story mansion with mansard roof and a tower like the pilot house of a coastal steamboat. The house had bathrooms with marble washbowls; central heat from a big coal burning furnace; a butler's pantry; dressed granite front stairs; an ell with rooms for cook and maids; a coach house, also with a mansard roof; a parlor running the length of one side of the building, with full length mirrors, a hardwood spring floor, and a grand piano for dances. Generally the piazza went around three sides of the house; the grounds well kept by Pat Dolan, were surrounded by an ornate picket fence, and a copper beech and an umbrella tree adorned the premises. Often one might see an iron deer, as well as an iron dog, on the property. In colloquial speech the iron dog was thought to be akin to the brass monkey, for on a tough winter day men said it was cold enough to affect various parts of his anatomy.

JANUARY THAW

A warm turn in mid-winter. The prevailing northwest winds that bring bitterly cold air from Hudson's Bay give way to mild southerly breezes that start down Bermuda way. We get warm, genial sunshine, the snow melts, and so does the rock-like ice that has been on the ground since just after Christmas. Everyone relaxes, green grass shows here and there, water runs in the brooks and gutters, and a man with any sense at all, realizing he is getting a southern vacation for nothing, can practically smell the palm trees and oleanders. But the thaw which many say is the only good thing about January, soon ends, the winds from the Polar ice cap again come whistling down from Canada, the mud freezes into mean ruts, and we button up our overcoats. Like as not a blizzard will be along before week is out, just to get us ready for February.

JORUM

The old term for a Big Drink. "Jorum" might refer to the mug or the drink itself. Generally the word described hard stuff; a man might order a jorum of rum, but never a jorum of milk.

JUNCTION

The place where topography and economics have decreed that two railroads shall meet. There grew a roundhouse, a station with lunch room, a small hotel, a settlement of houses, a store, a bowling alley, and sometimes, bit by bit a town that has become the metropolis of the valley. When the up train pulls in and then the down train, and after that the "accommodation" from off the branch and a mixed train from a line coming down from the logging country, there is a great commotion at the Junction; hustling of mail bags and express, hurrying passengers, orders for the crews, refueling of locomotives. It is soon over, the trains depart, the station is quiet, and from around the mountain floats on the country air the long, faraway music of Sixty One's whistle as the man at the throttle gives Brown's Crossing two long and two short and one extra for good measure.

KEARSARGE NO. 3

 The famous steam fire engine sent by Portsmouth, New Hampshire to Boston in November 1872 in response to the call for out of town aid to fight the conflagration sweeping the city. Coming down by special train, the Kearsarge engine was rushed from the railroad yards to Washington and Milk Streets by a hundred men on the dead run. The buildings on the south side of Milk Street were a fiery inferno, the flames were reaching across the narrow thoroughfare and the steeple of the Old South Church, smoking and smouldering, seemed about to burst into flames. The Portsmouth steamer,

93

a powerful new Amoskeag, joined the fight, she alone could throw water to that height, her stream reached to the top of the church tower, cascading sheets of water down the exposed side of the spire. A great cheer roared up from the crowd. The beautiful church was saved for later generations and the fire turned away from the whole area north of Milk Street. The flames swept on to the harbor front, but on this flank the firemen were successful. Although steam fire engines continued to be built for more than forty years after Kearsarge No. 3's brilliant battle, she, as she fought that night, came very near representing perfection in the design and performance of this type of apparatus. Rugged, yet of graceful beauty, she did duty in her own home town for many decades after Boston's disaster, and today is preserved in the Fire Engine Museum at South Manchester, New Hampshire.

KELP

A broad leafed variety of sea weed growing on a stem often several feet long, found in abundance in the waters along the Yankee Coast and on the beaches at low tide. Rich in all plant foods, it is a valuable fertilizer made use of by prudent farmers and many deeds to farms within teaming distance of salt water have a clause granting a right of way to a certain beach for the purpose of hauling sea weed. Iodine, an element of value in the human diet, is present in these marine growths. New Englanders, who love to complain about their difficult climate and the ailments it visits upon them, rarely pause to consider that the trace of iodine in the fish they eat and the crops raised on land fertilized by sea weed makes them practically free of goitre, a serious affliction common among inland people. The incidence of goitre is somewhat diminished in our day, for modern refrigeration makes it possible for a fresh fish from Gloucester to reach the table of a lady in Kokomo in fairly passable condition.

KINDLING WOOD WAGON

A one horse affair, lightly built but with front, rear and sides seven or eight feet high and a small aperture in the rear, at the bottom, with a sliding door. Perched on his seat the driver let his horse plod up and down the streets of the town, while he intoned the word "Wood" in a key which carried his message to every corner of the neighborhood. When a housewife whose kindling pile was low flagged him down, he hopped off his seat, set his two bushel basket at the rear of his wagon, opened the slide and let the fresh cut pine edgings run out until the basket was full. With his load on his back he trotted into the yard again and again until his customer's wood box was full, collected his money and drove on, intoning his word; prolonging it and managing to attain a musical note that satisfied his inner being. No sooner was he gone than the boys retrieved any small pieces of fresh cut pine left in the street. Some liked to whittle a piece, some liked to carry it in a pocket along with the numerous other small objects they had found and saved, so they might take it out from time to time, and smell the redolence of the freshly sawn wood. With the oil burners of today there is little demand for kindling wood and the man with the tall sided wagon and the load of pine edgings and the musical call has driven his shaggy old horse around the last bend in the road.

KNOW

"I wouldn't know him from a side of sole leather." The old time shoemakers used this expression, a "side" being one half of a cow's hide.

"I'd know him if I saw his hide in a tan yard." Another shoemaker's expression, this one not indicating a favorable opinion of the person mentioned, since there appears to be implicit the thought that the speaker hopes to see this person's hide in a tan yard.

"I wouldn't know him from Adam's off ox." The old timers knew, of course, this meant the right hand ox in Adam's yoke. It was alliteration only, that won for the off ox, rather than the nigh one, a place in this expression.

KULCH

Synonymous With Rubbidge.

LESLIE'S RETREAT

 An episode that nearly started the American Revolution. In late February 1775 General Gage sent Colonel Leslie and his 64th Regiment by ship to Marblehead with orders to land, march the five miles to Salem and seize the guns and ammunition collected by the American patriots. While the drums rolled to warn the Marbleheaders the Redcoats were coming ashore, Major Pedrick galloped to Salem to give the alarm. Colonel Pickering and his Minute Men managed to get all the cannon and gun powder casks across the North River and when the British regiment arrived the draw bridge was up and a few Colonial troops were lined up on the far bank, ready to fight. The word had been passed through the countryside and from towns as far away as Haverhill the Minute Men hurried for Salem with their muskets and powder horns. Colonel Leslie demanded that the draw bridge be lowered and Colonel Timothy Pickering, commanding the Americans, shouted back his defiance. To force a crossing meant a pitched battle, bloodshed, the beginning of war. This Leslie knew, and he also knew that he faced court martial unless he carried out his orders. Salem men with axes were smashing up the boats with which he might cross and he ordered his troops to bayonet them. Here Rev. Thomas Barnard, minister of Salem's North Church, intervened. From Leslie he managed to obtain a promise that if the

98

bridge were lowered, he would march his regiment no more than 30 rods on the other side. From Pickering he got a promise to withdraw his constantly growing horde of Minute Men 30 rods. So down came the bridge, the British marched the distance and then it was "about face" and back to their ship lying off Marblehead with drums thumping and the fifes playing "The World Turned Upside Down." In Marblehead, Colonel Glover's regiment stood silently in formation as the British passed, which doubtless convinced Leslie he had acted wisely.

LIAR'S BENCH

The settee in front of a country store, usually on the verandah where folks who could spare anywhere from five minutes to all day took their ease, exchanged news, swapped yarns, chewed tobacco and did a little business. No radio in those days, no local journal, and few saw the Boston papers, so an opportunity to hear what the other fellow was doing filled a need in the lives of those living on widely spaced farms. On the bench the weather was discussed and reviled, crops and critters and prices came in for a thorough working over, the number of points on the buck George Perkins shot over Goshen way was argued and George's veracity thoroughly thrashed out. The man who claimed he saw a panther on Knob Mountain while cutting cord wood received acrid advice about visiting an oculist; various ailments, from Quincy sore throat to tape-

99

worm, had their full measure of thought and study, and politics were always in order. One sitting on the bench while the Union Army was trying to take Richmond could have heard a better plan than Grant's. In 1898 he could have known the facts of the Battle of Manila Bay as well as if he had been on the "Olympia". Later still, he could have learned the one sure way of breaking the German trench line on the old Western Front and who was to blame for the Pearl Harbor disaster. Today people may draw up to the store in motor cars, have radio and television and prompt newspaper delivery and be in much closer touch with each other, but the bench is still there and it is still the place where great issues are discussed and settled.

LIE LIKE A TOMBSTONE

By this expression the old timers meant a falsehood that speaks too well of someone or something rather than too ill. Flattering fibs may appeal to some, but the New Englander is a blunt fellow, suspicious of any man who tries to upgrade him or anyone else beyond what he truly deserves. This expression is derived from inscriptions on old time gravestones, usually from the Scriptures or of a religious nature. Matter of fact Yankees, reading and at the same time recalling the character of the deceased whom they knew so well, often decided the inscription was a lie carved in marble. "He gave full measure" on the stone of a storekeeper who watered the milk, sanded the sugar and put sawdust in the coffee did not impress the neighbors who read it. Nor did the words "Asleep in Jesus" on a tombstone convince them that the smug deacon who every so often used to take the Boston train for a weekend with a lady in Scollay Square was not elsewhere than encamped for all Eternity with the Old Boy of the cloven hooves.

LIGHT PIE

The old timers referred to the entrails of an animal sometimes as "innards", sometimes as "liver and lights." Of all the creature's interior mechanism, only the liver had commercial value. "Lights" referred to everything else in there, and in old fashioned slaughtering it all was generally buried forthwith in a field that needed fertilizing. But not always, for those were hard scrabble days and many a Yankee farmer hard put to it to get by, selected some of the innards and handed them over to his good woman so she might disguise this collection as best she could in a pastry called "light pie." The farm wife did well with this difficult assignment and many a large Yankee family was brought up on a diet in which "light pie" was of frequent appearance. The boy who left the farm to go to the city to make his fortune and found the going mighty tough was able to take his hard circumstances the more philosophically because this dish did not appear on the boarding house menu.

LINE STORM

Rugged northeast gales that come roaring up the coast, about the time of the September and the March equinoxes. The wind drives the rain right out straight, we find new leaks in the roof and sometimes in the walls; blinds bang; small craft drive ashore and get stove up on the rocks; umbrellas get turned inside out; hats blow off and roll down the street, fetching up underneath some automobile; no one can keep a crease in his pants on such a day, and we get a few floods — usually minor but occasionally the real thing. Generally after one of these equinoctial gales, the wind backs into the northwest after a day of this sort, and we have a bright blue sky and a chance to dry out. The March line storm sometimes is a blizzard, leaving us a foot or more of snow, which isn't too bad; it's just more of the same, we are used to it, and we are soon rid of it. Moreover, it gives the ski tows a little extra business. The September line storm has turned out to be a full hurricane several times, and there is nothing meaner, particularly where we never used to have winds that would pick off a roof and drop it down the road a piece.

LOGGERHEAD

An iron rod with a small iron knob on one end. Heated, it was thrust into a bowl of flip or cider or rum to impart the burned taste so much fancied by the copper bellies of earlier days. Flip, then a popular drink, could be whiskey, beer or wine; the choice generally depending upon which liquor was most readily available.

Is also used to mean an upright post in a whaleboat around which the men could take a turn after they had harpooned a whale and the line was running out too fast. If they thus checked the outrunning line, they got a fast trip behind an eighty ton whale, an experience not easily forgotten. See "Nantucket Sleigh Ride." The word can mean a head that is thick (or stupid), hence the phrase "to be at loggerheads" with someone; i.e. quarrelling or in opposition.

LONG BOAT

The largest and most able of a ship's boats, often used for going ashore for firewood or water. In abandoning ship the long boat was the safest and most likely to survive. Old mariners, if about to withdraw from a difficult situation, would say, "I'll take the long boat and go ashore."

LONG HOME

This was where a mortal goes when his terrestrial life tenancy is terminated, according to the old timers. The word "long" did not refer to the dimensions of the hereafter, but rather to the length of one's stay therein. Nor did the old Yankees presume to say whether one departed was with the angels within the pearly gates, enjoying optimum climatic conditions and boundless opportunities, or whether he was in the perpetually sultry regions where the Old Nick presides over those doomed to discomfort and frustration. About the year 1800 one of our consuls, reporting to the State Department the decease of the Sultan of Morocco, a ruler responsible for the enslavement of many American mariners states simply that this Prince of Barbary had gone to his "long home." This indicated thorough acceptance by the consul of the command "judge not," for if ever an old Yankee selected some one to spend eternity in the hot place, he would choose one of the pirate chieftains of the Barbary Coast.

LONGER THAN A WET WEEK

The New Englander has in mind one of those weeks when it seems as if the sun has forgotten him, it drizzles, sometimes it pours, then it is just cloudy, the leaves drip, the birds have no song. Clothes mildew in the closet, boards warp, it is too wet to work in the garden and everyone is cranky. Then, after this long dreariness, comes a day when the wind manages to get out of the wet corner and a northwest breeze breaks the clouds until one may see a blue patch large enough to make a Dutchman a pair of breeches. Time now to stop being grumpy.

LOST HIS BEARINGS

A phrase descriptive of a man uncertain as to what decision to make, what direction to take. It comes to us from the old time mariners, who, when approaching a coast always looked for a landmark, a well known object. Once a skipper sighted a lighthouse, or church steeple or odd shaped hill, he knew from his chart or from what other shipmasters had told him, the compass bearing it should have if he were to sail in safe water. Perhaps his directions might tell him to keep a stone beacon southwest by south until he sighted a white house on a bluff, then steer northeast a half north until he raised the fort, and follow the channel markers into the harbor. When by reason of fog or storm or darkness a sea captain lost his bearings, he immediately shortened sail, hove to and dropped anchor. To do otherwise was to chance going aground on a sandbar or piling up on a ledge. So in other walks of life, a man who has metaphorically lost his bearings, drops anchor and waits for the weather to clear, thus following the old Yankee maxim that says "When you don't know what to do, do nothing."

MACKEREL SKY

A pattern of equally spaced narrow white clouds with blue sky showing in between, not unlike the regular markings on the skin of a mackerel. Those who think they can foretell the weather by the various cloud formations and other signs say "mackerel sky, never long wet, never long dry." According to Mark Twain "never long wet, never long dry" is a safe prediction at any time in these parts. Brought up in the middle west, he vainly tried to get used to the weather here, but he gave up and coined his immortal epigram "If you don't like New England weather, just wait a minute." He continued to reside here, however.

MAIL CRANE

A four by four upright standing just beyond a small up-country railroad station. Two horizontal arms extend from the upright toward the track and the outgoing mail bag, tied in the middle so it looks like an hour glass, is rigged between the two projecting arms. The station agent waits, usually accompanied by a half a dozen who want to see the limited highball through town. They hear the engineer whistle for a crossing miles away; silence, then a faint rumble before he is even in sight, the noise grows louder, he comes around the bend and heads down the long stretch of straight track toward the station, swaying and rocking along at full speed; black smoke streaming back over the cars, the drumming of the engine's exhaust swelling into a roar. In the mail car door, a clerk, watching through a tiny windshield, swings the arm of the "catcher" out as the train bullets through, the steel bar connects with the narrow middle of the mail bag, snatches it from the crane and holds it so the man can swing it inside. A split second before the catcher plucks the outgoing mail from the crane, the clerk heaves the incoming bag, and, if he is a good shot, it lands in front of the telegraph office and scuffs across the board platform. Working steam, the engineer staring straight ahead, the locomotive is through the station and gone in a blur of flashing rods and dust and smoke. The business of the mail clerk is done so fast it is hard to see what happens, the Pullmans whisk by, the diner with its broad windows and white table cloths and passengers calmly eating chicken salad or broiled scrod, then the coaches, and on the rear platform the brakeman, waving. The station agent waves back to let the brakeman know he sees no hot boxes or other trouble along the train. Everyone on the platform watches the express grow smaller in the distance and when the last car has rounded the hill and the man at the throttle is giving her two long and two short and one extra for that crossing where they hit a gravel truck two years ago, the postmaster picks up the incoming mail bag, tosses it into his car and drives up to the village.

MAPLE SUGAR

One of old Mother Nature's choicest gifts to those who have the stamina to winter in the New England hill country. When the days are brighter and the light is kindlier and the snow begins to melt and there are foam flecked pools in the brooks, the maple trees awake from their long, cold sleep, the sap climbs slowly through myriad capillaries — up through the trunks to the branches above—reaching for the sun. Then the first activity of the new season begins. A boy jabs his knife into a big maple in the grove on the sunny side of the hill and sees moisture follow his blade. He runs for the house, slipping and sliding over the corn snow of early spring, bursts into the kitchen and shouts "sap's runnin'". His father takes his feet out of the oven, lays down his pipe and gets busy. By nightfall the spouts are in the trees, a bucket hanging on each one, and the farmer has ranged through his "sugar bush," noting which of the younger trees have come along enough to be bored this year. Thereafter, for short weeks, everyone carries buckets full of sap, suspended from shoulder yokes, the ox team or perhaps a tractor hauls a sledge with tubs of the liquid over the snow to the sap house, a wood fire blazes continually under the enormous shallow pan and, by evaporation, the precious maple syrup is manufactured. With further time over the fire, it may be reduced to maple sugar. Everyone is in the woods while the sap is running, busy carrying or helping with the critters, or feeding wood into the fire or bottling the syrup. A sugaring off party in the snow is part of it, and then before one knows it, the sun has climbed still higher in the sky, the maple buds are bursting and dropping their husks on the old snow and the season is over. Vermont is the king of maple sugar, but in Maine and New Hampshire, the Berkshires and northeastern New York, the farmers share in the liquid gold of the season's first crop.

MARCH

It comes in like a lion and goes out like a lamb, we have said from the time the first settlers became acquainted with New England's exasperating yet interesting climate. That is, of course, as it should be. In early March Old Man Winter is in retreat, fighting a desperate rear guard action. Although the sun rides higher in the heavens, Winter's cavalry comes storming down out of the Northland with gales from the region of Hudson's Bay and snow and freezes. In a year when the forces of Spring seem stronger than usual and Winter seems to have acknowledged defeat, the true Yankee is uneasy, even though green grass, the crocus and the forsythia are here. The enemy is crafty, they well know, quite capable of charging in with icy winds or a howling blizzard and freezing up everything; the trusting flowers and the buds, the folks who too soon laid away long underwear and the automobile radiators with insufficient alcohol. So we say that if March comes in like a lamb, it goes out like a lion. In some years the Yankee has to go through this sort of thing even after March should be dead and buried. Of such a season he says that this year their will be six weeks sleighing in April.

MOROCCO SHOP

A term generally applied to tanneries specializing in the processing of goatskins, either by the use of chrome or of sumac. First used by the Moors of

North Africa, the method of tanning goatskins was named for their country, "Morocco." Most of the skins for Yankee tanneries were brought in ships from faraway places; cowhides from Spanish California and the Argentine, goathides from Arabia and East Africa. A tanner opening up a bale of goatskins always had an eye out for something interesting such as a pelt of a leopard folded into the center by some Arab trader to bulk out his merchandise a bit. For a classic account of the Californian cowhide trade, see Dana's masterpiece, "Two Years Before the Mast."

MUSTACHE CUP

Across the top was a concave piece of china in which the luxuriant mustache so prized by the 19th century male could rest while he was drinking tea or coffee. The top was open except for this piece of china; on one side being a space large enough to admit a man's mouth and on the other a wider opening through which to fill the cup. Until this invention a man often draped his mustache in his coffee, spoiling its appearance, changing its color, affecting the flavor of his drink, and, if he was not very careful, spotting his shirt front.

NANTUCKET SLEIGH RIDE

The term was made famous by the Nantucket islanders, who, in the first half of the 19th century, made fortunes from whales caught in the far oceans of the world. When the mast-head lookout sighted the spouting of a whale, he shouted "Thar she blows," the boats were lowered away and rowed to the spot, the man in the bow of the first boat to reach the whale threw his harpoon and when it sank into the creature, things began to happen fast. The whale might "sound," that is, he might go deep. Or he might thrash about on the surface, smashing the whaleboat. Or he might run for it, in which case the harpooner would let out all the line in his tubs, take a double bight around the loggerhead and let the whale tow the boat at a wild speed until he was tired out. The oarsmen would rest on their oars, while the boat went through the water at terrific speed, shipping spray over the bow and leaving a boiling wake astern. Sometimes the boat caught a wave and foundered, or took aboard so much water that the line had to be cut, but generally the "Nantucket sleigh ride" ended when the whale wore himself out many miles away from the ship. Then the whale might react savagely, but the Nantuckers never hesitated, for their watchword was "a dead whale or a stove boat."

NIGHT MAIL

Everywhere in rural New England this is the name given the through train that rattles across the countryside during the hours of darkness with its sleeping cars, mail, express, a smoker and a coach with a few dozing lumberjacks and college boys traveling cheap, and perhaps a milk car or two on the head end. One terminus of the run may be Montreal or Fort Fairfield or Halifax or Albany, but the other is always Boston. There are a few minutes of activity under the dim lights of an up-country station platform when the night mail pulls in. A weary traveling man gladly seeks the comfort of a Pullman berth, someone gets out of the coach and looks around to see if anyone is there to meet him, express packages are tossed out onto a waiting truck and the mail sacks sail through the air, landing in the cinders by the station. Milk cans rattle, people in the sleeping cars wake up, grumble, and turn over, the conductor shouts at the station agent, the air goes off with a long stuttering sigh, the engineer cracks the throttle and the night mail gets out of town, rumbles over the bridge and gathers speed for the long grade ahead. The man on the right side of the cab pulls the whistle cord — two long and two short — for a crossing, and an extra whoop if the road has a blind turn, and folks in farmhouses for miles in every direction hear the lonesome echo over the hills, a long deep faraway musical note unlike anything else in the world. By its sound in the night

112

they know what time it is, and where the wind is and that all is well. If they have lived in those parts for a spell, they may even know by the whistle's sound who is at the throttle that night.

OFF SOUNDINGS

 A sailor's term meaning well out to sea. A ship is "off soundings" when she is far enough at sea so she is beyond the relatively shallow waters of the Continental Shelf where it is possible to use the lead line to ascertain depth. Mariners put great reliance on the depth of the water to determine the ship's position, and they put tallow on the lead so it will bring up mud or sand or tiny shells to show them what the ocean floor is like. An experienced captain knows the depths and the characteristics of the bottom of the sea in coastal waters so thoroughly that by his soundings on a foggy night he gets a good idea of where he is. When he is "off soundings" he must wait until the weather clears and he can "shoot the sun" before he may determine the ship's position.

ON THE HIND TIT

The language some people who are given to earthy metaphor use to express the idea they are not getting as much as they are entitled to. They say "I'm always on the hind teat," the analogy being to a litter of pigs have a feeding from the mother pig (sow), and

113

the idea is that those up front are doing much better than the last one in line. The notion that whether a little pig is forward, aft or amidships while taking sustenance has anything to do with the quantity of the nourishment he receives is quite without any scientific basis. Nevertheless the idea persists among the uninformed, and this analogy, inaccurate as it is, continues in current use. Another notion is that the last pig in the litter is weak and pindling and probably will not thrive. To him is applied the term "teatman," perhaps because it is thought he has a hard time of it finding a place for himself at meal time. However, the teatman often turns out to be the best of the litter, and so it is with other creatures, as the fable of the Ugly Duckling teaches us.

ORTS

An old fashioned word for table scraps. Shakespeare has a line; "let him have time a beggar's orts to crave." This word, like its synonym "swill," has gradually died out as folks have sought more refinement of speech through the use of more syllables, and the term "garbage" is now more commonly accepted, although the truly cultured achieve the ultimate in polysyllabic respectability with the expression "culinary residuum."

OVER TO THE CONTINENT

The expression the inhabitants of Nantucket use when they refer to that other part of the continent of North America not included within the limits of their island. Sometimes they go "over to the continent" to transact business with folks on the mainland," whom they term "off islanders," whether they are the people of Wellfleet or Hyannis or New Bedford or New York. A man from Truro would be an "off islander," so would a man from Boston or Chicago or Vancouver or any other part of "the continent." In the old days a Nantucketer leaving his island would be more likely bound for a three year stay at sea aboard a whaler than for a sojourn of even one day on North America or any other continent.

PARLOR STOVE

 A small wood burner, prettily decorated with nickel trim, setting in the family's "front room." In the days before a furnace in the cellar and a central heating system using hot air, steam or hot water, almost every room had its own stove connected to one of the several chimneys that a fair sized house had. While the parlor stove was no different structurally, it was a better finished and more refined piece of equipment, since it was in the best room in the house along with the plush rocking chairs, the horsehair sofa, the Rogers Group, the marble top table and the stuffed pheasant under a glass dome. Hard coal, as it became more common, replaced wood as fuel in more prosperous urban homes, yet in some

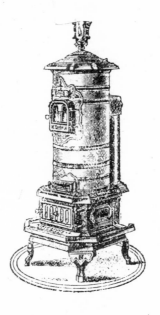

parts of northern New England, where the forest is near at hand and the man of the house is in good health, the stove in the front room even today runs on oak, birch, beech and maple. Such stoves are the stage in the development of house heating that followed the shallow and efficient open fireplace in each room. The open faced Franklin stove and then the round "airtight" stove followed and the fireplaces were often boarded over, a hole being left for the stove pipe. After the stoves came the hand fired furnace in the cellar and then automatic oil heat.

PARSNIPS

The Yankees say "that butters no parsnips" when they think some one is giving them a fast game of talk.

PARSON'S NOSE

Alias "the part that went over the fence last;" a protuberance on the stern of a fowl or turkey, heart shaped and about the size of a walnut. It is a continuation of the backbone and is the bird's real tail, the feathers being merely an appendage. Technically the "parson's nose" is composed of the pygostyle, which is the last of the vertebra of the backbone, and the elaeodochon or rump gland, which contains oil. A bird presses its bill against the elaeodochon, thus getting a drop of oil and then "preens" or dresses its feathers. Disposal of the "parson's nose" is a problem on Thanksgiving Day, and it is the only part of the turkey which certainly will leave the table intact. Nor does it accommodate itself to incorporation in a turkey sandwich over the weekend. In restaurants the disposition of the "parsons nose" is less of a problem, for there is always the soup kettle.

PATENT ROCKER

A rocking chair set upon a low frame so that its rockers, instead of being upon the floor, rest upon two horizontal wooden members. Under the seat, front and rear, are two heavy coil springs to cushion and check the forward and backward motion so whoever is enjoying the chair will not rock the whole affair in too wide an arc and fetch up on the floor. The patent rocker is a refinement given us in the Victorian era, a time when the sedate and genteel was more sought after than before or since. Many who know and love rocking chairs feel that the inventor of this device tried to gild the lily; others hold that in the squeak of the springs as one rocks is a companionable and comforting note, particularly for a person alone in the house, waiting for someone who is coming home, or for someone who is not.

PEA IN A HOT SKILLET

When natives of these parts wish to describe a person who is extremely active, they say he is "jumping around like a pea in a hot skillet." Some folks who are fond of the picturesque have other words they substitute for "pea" in this expression.

PEA SOUP FOG

Weather so thick a lobsterman with his hand on the tiller cannot see the bow of his dory. The sound of the bell buoy is far away in the blank, gray-white mist. As if from nowhere one hears gentle waves washing up on invisible rocks; disembodied voices from another boat float across the water; the putt-putt of a motor hangs in the still air. Ashore motorists crawl along with their lights on in the daytime, and if it is after dark, they may count themselves fortunate if they don't get lost. On such a day a Gloucesterman, whose house stood at the harbor's edge, was repairing his roof and shingled right off into the fog. He kept on shingling until his hammer struck the foremast of a schooner getting ready to sail for the Grand Banks, and then he slid down a backstay, and signed aboard.

PEPPER

To most people only a condiment in a fancy box on the pantry shelf, but to a New Englander living in one of the old seacoast towns the word means sailing ship voyages to the Indies in the old days, rich pepper cargoes from Sumatra, tall white mansions built by prosperous merchants, ancestral legends of Oriental typhoons and battles with Malay pirates. For years after Jonathan Carnes, in 1797, discovered a plentiful source of pepper in Sumatra, Salem was the world center of the trade. Other local ports shared in the business and made money selling pepper to the Mediterranean countries. Prior to the time Carnes found he could buy the berries directly from the natives, the business had been a Dutch monopoly, supplies were limited and prices high. Demand was strong, for in those days refrigeration did not exist and pepper was one of the important meat preservatives. Illustrating its efficacy is the story of the old Salem merchant obsessed with the fear of being buried alive. He exacted from his family the promise that his body would not be interred until thirty days after the doctor opined he was dead. Although he passed away in July, and it was a hot summer, the family had no problem, for they packed the coffin with pepper berries and he lay in the front room in a very presentable state until the thirty days were up. Then they conveyed him to his tomb, where he lay for more than a century until his descendants had occasion to repair the stonework. The coffin cover being rotted, it was replaced, and then they discovered he was still in a perfect state of preservation in his eternal bed of pepper berries. His appearance was little different than in the oil painting done not long before his passing, still in the family's possession and hanging in the drawing room of the mansion he had built on Chestnut Street in Salem.

PERAMBULATE THE BOUNDS

This procedure, required by statute, has been followed since earliest colonial times. On a day agreed upon the Selectmen of the town meet with the officials of the towns (or cities) adjoining and together they examine the boundary markers separating their respective municipalities to ascertain that they are properly situated. There is less possibility of dispute these days, since the bounds have been long established, but in the earlier days of sparse settlements occasionally markers were moved in the dark of the moon so a few likely tracts of real estate might be added to the town. Today the procedure reminds officials of the limits of their own jurisdictions, so they will not be sending their police and firemen to do work in the other fellow's town or try to collect taxes from owners on the other side of the line. When the Selectmen and city councillors of the various communities have made sure no one has stolen any territory, they adjourn to a place of public refreshment.

PERCH POLE

A stick used by the old timers for measuring land, especially in woodlots and hill pastures where the terrain is rough and the distances considerable. A "perch" is 5½ yards (16½ feet) and in old deeds is more commonly called a "rod." In a title search, an old deed is sometimes found measured in perches or rods, rather than in feet. When a man was going to sell a "parcel" of land in the old days before steel tapes, he would reach down his perch pole from the cross ties of the wagon shed and go out on the land with the buyer. Beginning at a stake and stones, they measured to a blasted pine, thence to a corner of the ledge, thence to the bend in the brook, thence along the thread of the brook to a stone wall, thence as the wall stands to the oak beside the pasture gate, thence by land now or formerly of the Widder Perkins to the point of beginning. Be all of said measurements more or less.

PERSNICKITY

Unusually fussy and particular about one's food and easily annoyed by things such as drafts, opposing political opinions, people who sing while taking a bath, and the smoke from a five cent cigar. Although a doctoral dissertation has been written on the derivation of this word, its origin still remains obscure.

PEYTON PLACE

A mythical town in New Hampshire somewhere north or west of Concord where the streams flow toward either the Merrimac or the Connecticut in which a stranger saw and recorded all manner of libidinous antics not visible to the naked eye. New Englanders previously unaware that their native land so closely resembled the twin cities of the plain, avidly perused this record. So did ladies across the country who love to read in cold print intimate details of intimacies. No one has located this mythical locality, but some think it is near the North Country town visited by an eminent Sociology Professor who sought to ascertain the reason for its extremely high birth rate. He learned nothing from most careful research until one native told him that the Night Mail, Boston bound, came barrelling through in the gray dawn, whistling two long and two short for several different crossings, waking everybody. Too early to get up and too late to go to sleep, explained the townsman. The Professor departed, confident

he had a scientific solution he could write up in an
article for a learned journal.

PINDLING

Small, ill nourished and not all thriving. Although
usually applied to a child who appears pale and thin,
the word is sometimes used to describe a calf or
chicken not coming along as it should.

POLE CAT TRAIL

On New England hills where snow is now a cash
crop and ski tows have been installed to haul the
city folks to the top of the mountain, there are two
types of trails. One is steep and fast, for those who
are not only young but expert on skis and a trip
to the bottom, down sharp pitches and around difficult turns, is an experience. This is known as the
"wild cat trail" and it is here the rescue crew picks
up casualties and sees to getting them to the local
hospital, where the plaster cast is fitted. The other
trail is slow, its slopes are gentle, its turns are on a
broad curve, the inexpert skier has easy spills and
his trip down the mountain is leisurely enough so
that he may glance at the scenery now and then.
Seldom do the orthopedic men get business from this
trail. This is the "pole cat trail," so named in honor
of Brother Skunk, who has made his leisurely way
about the New England scene since time immemorial,
never hurrying. With the matter of speed the anal-

ogy ends. On the "pole cat trail" the inexpert skier goes slowly in order to be safe. On the other hand, the pole cat himself goes slowly because he knows he is safe; he knows he has for any creature who presumes to interrupt his gentlemanly progress, a consignment of the ne plus ultra of all stinks. Neither man nor beast ever meddles with Brother Skunk but once. So the Yankee uses the term pole cat here to denote sedate and dignified progress.

POOR MAN'S MANURE

An early spring snowfall of an inch or two that melts gradually when the sun comes out, giving all its moisture to the top soil. This is thought to be more beneficial to the land than an ordinary rain, which may run off quickly, eroding the field and leaving only part of its moisture for the ground. This notion that spring snow is a boon to the man who cannot afford extra loads of "dressing" is an example of Yankee optimism.

POTATO BARGAIN

A dish well known to old Cape Codders. Fry out 3 slices of fat salt pork in an iron spider, remove the pork and when the fat is cool, add 7 potatoes, peeled, halved and sliced, and 4 medium sized onions, peeled, sliced and cooked separately, salt and pepper to taste. Cover with water to within $3/4$ inch from top of spider, bring to boiling point and cook until potatoes are done. When water is partly boiled away, place whole slices of bread on top, put on a cover and steam them along with the potatoes and onions for 15 minutes. Then serve to folks who really need calories, and if you cannot lick the high cost of living with this one, you never will.

POUND

Here and there in New England the traveler who looks sharp may see a tiny square pasture shaded by a great elm and enclosed by a wall of gray and mossy stones that plainly has stood for centuries. This is the "Town Pound" in which, by statute law, the field driver was directed to place any stray horse, cow, sheep or swine. There the critters stayed, fed and watered, until the owner appeared and paid the field driver the fees which the law provides he shall have for each impounded animal. In the old days, when New England was a land of many farms, the pound keeper's job was of vital importance, for cultivated fields can be ruined by stray cattle or pigs and it was very necessary that they be confined. His post was profitable, too, for the upland pastures supported a great number of domestic animals and they were always getting out. Today, except for the valley lands, what was once field and pasture has again been claimed by the forest, the field driver rarely functions and the town pound, its grass ungrazed, is only a feature for amateur photographers and folks with a set of oil paints.

PRIVY

Synonymous with BACKHOUSE. For technical data see that title. The word privy indicates a degree of privacy and is one of several attempts by those of an earlier day to arrive at a respectable name for the very necessary little building out back. In hotels and other multiple occupancies, one was called the "Gents Walk" and the other the "Ladies Walk," it being assumed no one would be in such case as to be obliged to run. The privy is by means obsolete today in many communities where the electric service is subject to interruption by storms. When the power fails, the electric pump does not fill the tank, householders are reminded that modern civilization is not yet wholly perfect, and a trip to the yard is indicated. On the chart of Salem Bay there appears in the area off Peach's Point, Marblehead, the legend "Privy Ledge." Historical research has not yet revealed the reason for thus naming this rock, although there is a theory that old time mariners located it and steered clear of it by taking a bearing on some privy ashore that stood in a place of prominence unusual for this type of structure.

PUCKERSNATCH

This term the old timers used to describe a hasty and unskillful job of sewing. The word, invented by some old lady with a penchant for pungent phrase, describes admirably both the appearance of the completed work on the garment and the motions of the person impatiently and hurriedly plying her needle.

PUMP AUGUR

A tool to bore holes an inch or more in diameter, its handle sometimes as long as eight feet. Used in the days when metal was scarce to make a hole in a block of soft (punkin) pine for the shaft of a pump. With a plunger fitted by a skillful man, a rod, a spout and a handle, the pump was ready to be lowered into the well, primed and put to work supplying the family and the livestock with water. When towns first built water systems, the pipes were of wood, bored by these long pump augurs. Below ground the pipes were well preserved and even today an excavation in a city street may bring to light an old wooden water pipe. Both the pipes and the pump augurs are now museum pieces.

PUNG

A long low slung sleigh with two sets of runners, the front set being on a pivot so a sharp turn may be made. The narrow runners are short and of light, open-frame construction, unlike the long, broad stout timber of heavy duty sledges. Pungs were used largely as delivery vehicles for grocery, milk and laundry men and were great fun to hook rides on, for a boy could put his feet in between the struts of the frame, resting them on the low runner only a couple of inches from the ground, and ride along, holding onto the side and ready to duck low or drop off when the driver profanely turned to flick his long whip toward the rear. Most drivers were tolerant, but when 6 or 8 boys were riding his rear runners, he had to do something.

PUNKIN

A large, round vegetable somewhat resembling a squash, valuable solely for making one of the nicest pies there is. Never used as one of the vegetables in a dinner, as is its cousin, the squash. Frequently grown right in the corn patch, it is one of the symbols of the New England Autumn and the poet said "when the frost is on the punkin," to mean we are getting on in the year. "He thinks he's some punkins" is said of a fellow who is thought to hold too good an opinion of himself. It is sweeter than the squash and in old times folks who could not afford sugar made "punkin molasses" for sweetening. The spelling "Pumpkin" is often used, and is even to be found in some dictionaries. The second letter "p" is silent, although occasionally people without a good background let it slip into their pronunciation of the word.

QUICK HITCH

 The harness for the horses of the old time fire engine, ready and hanging by a stout cord from the ceiling of the fire station. When the tapper hit, with staccato blows counting out an alarm on the big gong over the desk, the well trained horses galloped from their stalls in the rear of the station and took their proper places under the harnesses. Men slid down the brass poles and came running across the house floor, one on each crew pulled the cord and the harnesses dropped onto the backs of the team for his engine. Snapping the collars, the man ran for the rear step, while the driver, already on his seat, shouted to his horses and the apparatus rolled. Firemen who knew their business accomplished all this in 30 seconds from the moment the alarm hit. Within that time, in a big house, ten horses were hitched up, and the steamer, the hose wagon, the chemical and the ladder were galloping down the street, bells ringing, the horses' hooves striking sparks from the cobble stones, the men struggling into their rubber coats and reaching for their helmets. This beautiful teamwork of horses and men has been gone for many years, supplanted by the motor fire engine that responds to one kick of the starter and never gets tired. More efficient are the motors, yet no fireman who worked with horses could help feel, when he looked at the empty stalls, that the romance of the firefighting game had vanished.

129

QUILTING BEE

A gathering of all a lady's friends to complete in one final burst of industry the quilt upon which she had been working for months. A quilting bee was the old time counterpart of the modern assembly line process. In her spare time the lady prepared the squares that were to be the covers of the quilt; sometimes all of one design — more often cut from odd pieces of cloth saved from her dressmaking. The cotton padding, carefully combed on long winter evenings, would be ready, too, and a quilting frame set upon the backs of chairs. Onto the frame went the lining, then the inside padding, over it another cloth lining and finally the gaily colored squares of cloth, already sewed together to the size desired. After that, the women stood around the frame, facing each other, and quilted the patchwork on, working their needles and their tongues at a great rate and trotting out their choice bits of gossip. Sometimes the little girls of the various families were made to sit on the floor under the frame to take the needles as they were thrust down through the quilt and push them up to the mothers working on the upper side. If it was a hot summer day and the hoop skirts of the busy ladies made too complete a wall around the quilting frame, a little girl might faint in the close atmosphere underneath and have to be hauled out and revived with cold lemonade. The women spent the day and had a big dinner and went home, all talked out, in time to get supper for their families. If they had done a good job, the quilt might win a prize at the County Fair, but it had to be well done, for there was plenty of competition.

RED FLANNEL HASH

 A picturesque term for just plain hash made by a cook who happens to have a few extra beets on hand to chop up and sling into the mixture. The rest of the recipe is standard operating procedure; some corned beef, onion, potato, turnip and seasoning. Ella's hash differs from Eliza's hash only in so far as the artist varies the proportions and chooses the various spices. A good dish of this stuff, well browned, is a fine meal, economical, filling and easy to make. Every Yankee restaurant serves either the Red Flannel or the White Flannel (without beets) variety, and a good job they do with it, except when the cook out back has an easy conscience and permits orts to sneak in that rightfully belong in the receptacle for the culinary residuum.

RIDE AND TIE

The method by which two men used one horse to reach a destination. The first man started off on horseback, rode a mile or so and tied the animal to a tree and then walked on. The second man, who set out on foot, untied the horse when he reached him, rode on past his companion and at the end of his mile tied up the steed and walked on. So the process went for whatever length their journey was;

not as swift or easy as if they both had horses, but this was in the days before every man had his own conveyance. The two riders ran the risk the horse might be stolen while tied, yet the risk was not great, for a thief could not get far and when caught, his punishment often was meted out on the spot.

ROCK HIM

And the refrain was "rock him round the corner" when the old time Marbleheaders saw a "foreigner" in town, and did not happen to like the cut of his jib. The "foreigner" was generally someone from nearby Salem or Lynn and if he had earned himself a "rocking," it usually was because he had presumed to pass an uppity remark to some Marbleheader. The men of Salem had always been their enemies since colonial days and as recently as 1939 a Salem lobsterman who dared come to Marblehead and sell his wares to summer residents a cent a pound cheaper got the treatment. Fleeing a hail of round beach stones, he was grateful when the Marblehead police intervened and immured him in the hoosegow at the old Town House in "protective custody." In the old days a man from Lynn was immediately distinguishable because of his overcoat. Any Marbleheader who saw such an undesirable in town shouted "jacket over a coat, he's a Lynner; rock him, rock him around the corner." And sentence was forthwith executed. Marblehead's rocks do not fly around nearly as much as they did, because these are quieter times and the town has grown tremendously, largely through the influx of "foreigners." However, let no one assume that it can't happen now.

ROOT CELLAR

An underground storage place on the farm for potatoes, beets, carrots, turnips and parsnips. Although it may be dug below grade, it is best to choose a side hill so the root cellar may have an upright door and be easier to get in and out of. Food stored here is safe against freezing, and if well located, there will be no damage from dampness. In summer weather the coolness of the ground provides the optimum temperature for the prevention of rot and spoilage. The root cellar was one of the principal means of preserving food before the advent of refrigeration.

RUDDLE

The attic of a house. In New England the ruddle or attic, is the place for things not presently needed but which may be useful someday, somehow, somewhere. Here one may expect to find anything from a genuine Benjamin Franklin signature to a suddenly needed chamber pot. The uniformed fireman who calls for the annual inspection never approves of the multitude of items of possible future value stacked in the ruddle and often gives a lecture, but does not have the slightest notion that these treasures are going to be thrown out.

SACRED COD

 The representation of a codfish, four feet eleven inches long and made of a single piece of pine, which hangs in the chamber of the Massachusetts House of Representatives in the State House on Beacon Hill, Boston, opposite the Speaker's rostrum. In the ancient State House hung a wooden codfish, destroyed by the fire that leveled the building in 1747. When the new structure, which still stands at the head of State Street, was built to replace the old, another wooden codfish was hung in the Chamber. This one disappeared during the British occupation, doubtless the prize of some redcoat. In 1784, when at last our new nation was firmly established, the codfish we have today was hung in the Legislative Hall. In 1798, when the fine new State House with the Bulfinch front was opened, the cod was conveyed thither with due reverence and in 1895 he was again moved, this time to the new and larger House of Representatives in the just completed wing. Upon this occasion the orators told of the prosperity the cod has brought to the state from earliest times, the commerce with Europe and the Indies based on salt fish exports that helped build up our seaports, the hundreds of sailors the fishing fleet has given the Navy. The sacred cod hangs there today, the symbol of an industry that continues to provide jobs for thousands. In the time since 1784 no disrespectful hand has ever touched him except those of some Harvard students who in 1933 sneaked in, put him in a bass fiddle case, and scuttled back to Cambridge with their trophy. The Commonwealth was rocked by the uproar over the theft. The people were outraged that anyone should trifle with their emblem. Some one, the Harvard Dean, or perhaps the police, explained to these callow lads that the cod really is sacred. No one was arrested and the fish was back at his moorings within the week. There he remains, shown by the guides of the State House tours as they explain to school children and visitors from far away that he is now and always has been one great source of the Commonwealth's strength.

SAIL WAGON

One of the pieces of fire apparatus used in the era of the hand tub and hose reel. The mission of the sail wagon's crew was to haul their sheets of ship's canvas off the kit, wet them, then hang them on the exposed sides of the structures next to the burning building and spread them over any nearby wooden shingle roofs endangered by sparks. This technique of fire fighting proved unsuccessful because of the immense labor involved in raising the sails and fastening them to the eaves so they would hang down the sides of the building. For this, and for laying the wet sails over a roof, the assistance of a ladder company was needed and they were often otherwise occupied. Moreover, the sail wagon boys had to persuade the pipe men of one of the hand engines

135

companies to take their stream off the main blaze occasionally and give the canvas a quick wetting or it would dry out and commence to burn, thus spreading the fire instead of checking it. The acrid arguments between engine men and the sail wagon crew resulted finally in the discontinuance of this method. It was found that a strong stream played upon the roof from time to time was better protection against sparks. If directed at the eaves, the water cascading down like a curtain kept the walls sufficiently cool so they did not ignite. Hand tubs, hose reel and ladder carriage all have their successors in today's motor fire apparatus, but the sail wagon's function has disappeared and mention of it in the old records is hard to find.

SALEM GIBRALTER

An old fashioned candy bar concocted by a lady named Spencer in the first part of the 19th century. Made in many flavors, it was wrapped in a fancy paper with an aristocratic twist at each end and peddled throughout the region from her one horse candy wagon. Shipmasters departing from Salem saw to it they had a few cases of Gibralters aboard to sell as a novelty in some faraway port. Another confection was called "Zanzibar" for the East African city with which Salem merchants used to do so much business, and candy sticks known as "Black Jacks" were made in every flavor known to Yankee urchins. Distinctively old Salem, these are all made today, wrapped in the old time style, and provide something new in the way of candy experience for the tourists from all over the country who flock to the city during the good weather months.

SALEM STATION

A great gray granite structure with two Gothic towers 75 feet high, tall mullioned windows and a massive arch from which trains issued forth to cross Washington Street and plunge into the blackness of the tunnel. Built in 1847 by the old Eastern Railroad, it was a picturesque part of Salem until 1954, when it was demolished in a grade crossing elimination project. In the old days a gate closed the huge archway except at train time, departures were announced by the ringing of a convent bell captured by the

Americans at the siege of Port Royal and the bell ringer was a one legged corporal, a veteran of the War of 1812. Later the busy crossing in front had three flagmen on duty at all times, waiting in a stone guard house for the train signal and when the electric bell sounded, they marched out into the street, blowing their whistles to halt traffic. Hawthorne, in his "House of Seven Gables," describes "the arched entrance, the spacious breadth, the airy height from floor to roof, partially filled with smoke and steam." He did not mention the pigeons dwelling high in the rafters that ruined the hat of many a traveler. Salem Station survived the great Conflagration of 1914, although at one stage of the fire a dynamite squad was ready to blow it up to check the spread of the flames. The wind veered, the fire passed south and the Station was saved for another 40 years, at last falling victim to dreary progress.

SALT BOX HOUSE

The ordinary man built a two and a half story house with rooms on each side of the front door, the same plan on the second floor. Later, if he prospered, he might enlarge by extending the rear slope of the roof down to the first floor level, thus providing extra rooms in back. This alteration, wholly practical, resulted in a long downward sweep of the roof that gave a house the graceful appearance of having grown in that particular spot. When it was realized how this happy expedient had improved the architec-

ture of an otherwise plain house, the design was
followed generally. Because the top of an old fashioned salt box for the table had about the same slope,
this design came to be called the "salt box house."
It is common in houses built in colonial times and
has been widely copied in recent years. Some say
that the long slanting roof of the salt box house was
thus made so the Arctic blasts of winter would ride
up the slope, over the ridge pole and away. This
scheme is embodied in the modern principle of

streamlining. A wind striking a vertical wall seeks every crack and blows in around the window sashes, thus making the building difficult to heat. The sloping roof design is said to be the only way that man has ever fooled old Boreas in this northern climate.

SALT HOSS

In the days of sail the crew thus referred to the salt beef issued them nearly every day as the principal item in their ration. On a long voyage fresh provisions could not possibly last for more than the first few days, since any refrigeration was wholly lacking. A vessel bound for Calcutta or around the Horn, or even to West Indies ports, therefore had to rely on salt provisions, ship's bread (hardtack), dried peas and beans, and molasses. The cook soaked the salt beef overnight in a tub called by the men the "harness cask," because they always insisted this meat was not beef at all, but the carcasses of tired old horses which had departed his life while hauling a heavy load up a steep grade. The main course aboard a windjammer has been memorialized in a famous old bit of drama, author unknown. The sailor picked up a piece of "salt hoss," addressing it thus:

"Old hoss, old hoss, what brought you here,
"From Sacarap to Portland Pier."

Another sailor, speaking for the deceased horse, promptly chimed in:

"I've carted stone this many a year,
" 'Till killed by blows and sore abuse,
"They salted me down for sailor's use,
"The sailors they do me despise,
"They turn me over and damn my eyes,
"Cut off my meat and scrape my bones,
"And pitch me over to Davy Jones."

SAND CARPET

In the old days, when any kind of a carpet large enough to cover an entire floor was prohibitively expensive, people along the Yankee Coast used clean beach sand to cover the parlor floor. A clever housewife drew geometrical designs, rosettes and anchors in the sand and then issued strict orders to the family to keep out of the parlor unless some special caller arrived. In that event the designs on the sand carpet had to be re-done the next day. The blue sands from the Ipswich and Gloucester beaches and black sands from Mackerel Cove in Beverly were prized for this work, for they furnished a contrast with the more common white varieties. In Marblehead, in a house occupied by two families, the lady in the second story had a sand carpet in her "best room," for many years; it sifted through the cracks between the boards, gradually filling the space between the upper and lower ceiling. One afternoon the lady downstairs was entertaining the minister, gravity finally took charge, most of the ceiling collapsed and several barrels of sand cascaded down into the place, covering hostess, guest and furniture. It was when the lady upstairs suggested other substances that would have made a worse mess of the room than sand that a coolness arose between the two tenants which persisted for years.

SAND SHAKER

As tall as a salt shaker, of greater diameter, usually made of wood and with a perforated top concave or "dished" so as to form a shallow saucer. Before the days of good and plentiful blotters, people shook fine sand on the ink to dry it. Then carefully the writer tilted the paper, poured the sand into the saucered top and shook the receptacle until the sand dropped back into the holes of the shaker. Thus they used the sand over and over again, for good ink sand was hard to come by. Rev. William Bentley of Salem in his famous diary describes a visit to Mackerel Cove in Beverly to get some of the well known black sand from the beach there for his shaker. Even today the same vein of black sand is to be found there. Sand shakers were used not only in New England, but universally as late as 1840. It is told of some of the old time Sultans of Turkey that they considered sand too plebeian a substance to use in drying their ink, so they put gold dust in their shakers. Some of their state documents in existence today, under a magnifying glass, reveal the shining particles of the gold dust applied to the royal signature when it was wet.

SCISSORS GRINDER

An itinerant who pushed a two wheeled cart mounting several grindstones of varied sizes His vehicle had two or three gongs of different pitches that were sounded by strikers connected to the wheels. A housewife, hearing the unmusical but distinctive timbre up the street, looked around the house for all the knives and scissors that needed an edge put on them and hailed the old fellow as he trudged by. Two legs to the rear of the wheels supported his cart when he set it down, he squirmed into a tiny seat, put a foot on the treadle that powered his grindstones and went to work on the cutlery. Water from a tomato can with a hole punched in it moistened the whirling surfaces as he worked and he was soon surrounded by a circle of children attracted by the keening sound of the metal on the stones. When he was through he collected a few small coins from the lady of the house, picked up the handles of his cart and ding-donged along, looking for more business. Today there is a man who sharpens scissors and knives and he will come if you hunt out his number in the telephone book. His equipment is in a truck, he has no gongs to herald his arrival in the vicinity and his fee is considerably larger than what the old fellow with the cart used to charge.

SCRIMSHAW

The art of carving the teeth and lower jawbone of the whale, practiced by Yankee sailors of the early

19th century. After the capture of a whale and the trying out of his oil, the crew might have long days of inactivity before the sighting of another. In this tedious interval the men carved designs on the whale ivory, competing with each other to see who could do the best. Scrimshawing prevented the idleness that is usually the seed-bed for quarrels aboard ship and a quarrel on a whaler, where a harpoon or a keen edged blubber spade is near at hand, can be a bloody business. Museums in New England seaports all have specimens of scrimshaw; needle cases, pie crimpers, ditty boxes and all manner of delicately carved pictures of whaling scenes, ships, and of women, — some in hoopskirts, some stark naked. This art form has preserved for us a history of the whaling industry which at its height employed 20,000 Yankee mariners.

SCURVY

A disease caused by lack of vitamin C in the diet, very common among sailors on long voyages in the days of sail. Fresh fruit and vegetables, available in the first weeks, became exhausted after the vessel was long at sea, so that rations were salt beef, salt pork, ship's bread (hardtack) dried beans and peas. Scurvy broke out unless the master managed to touch at a port where fresh provisions were available. Loss of strength, muscular pains, shrunken gums, and foul breath characterized this ailment, the sailor was too weak to leave his bunk and often death resulted. In Dana's classic TWO YEARS BEFORE THE MAST, the ship bound from California around Cape Horn to Boston ran out of fresh food in the first weeks of the long voyage and by the time she had reached the West Indies, northward bound, she had several bad cases of scurvy. Luckily she spoke a small vessel plying between the islands that could sell them freshly dug potatoes and a few bags of onions. The cook crushed the new potatoes with mortar and pestle and fed the juice to the scurvy patients, by now too weak to eat solid food. Gradually they recovered and were back on duty before the ship reached Boston. The other sailors, vitamin starved, carried raw onions in their pockets, munching them as they went about their duties on deck. So when the vessel reached Boston, all aboard had been restored by the simple remedy of fresh vegetables. The British solved the scurvy problem by requiring that every ship issue lime juice to the men when the supply of fresh fruit and vegetables was exhausted. From this came the old Yankee term "Limey," which meant any Britisher from His Majesty the King down to the cabin boy on a Thames River Barge.

SEA ROOM

A large enough area in which to navigate a ship. In the age of steam this is not as much of a problem, for the skipper can plot his course and steer it, his only worry that the action of the tide or the wind might give his vessel enough drift to fetch him up on a shoal or mudbank. If he is in coastal waters, he is all right as long as he has power and keeps a sharp lookout. Not so with the master of a sailing ship. Always he had to see to it that if the wind suddenly shifted and became foul for his course, he had room to beat to windward. That means a series of tacks and reaches; long zig-zags into the eye of the wind. To do that requires plenty of "good water," where no rocks or shoals or capes or islands prevent him from sailing the long courses necessary to execute this difficult maneuver. Therefore a good shipmaster in the days of the windjammers always saw to it he had plenty of "sea room" so he would not be caught inshore, unable to bring his vessel about without piling her up. No lee shore was more feared than Cape Cod in the neighborhood of Highland Light. Many a captain made it safely all the way from Calcutta or Canton, only to lose his ship because he was in a hurry to get home, followed the coast too closely and then ran into an easterly blow without enough sea room to claw off.

SEA SERPENT

This critter from eighty to a hundred feet long, has cavorted about off the Yankee Coast from time to time over the years. His enormous ugly head is like that of a snake or alligator and he rears it up several feet above the water, thrusting forth his forked tongue, as he moves on the surface with an undulating motion, churning the water with a tre-

mendous foaming and splashing as he goes. On his back are regularly spaced bunches or humps which appear as he ripples along. Sea serpents have been seen along the Maine coast, in Long Island Sound, off Nahant and in 1817 upon numerous occasions in the waters around Gloucester chasing schools of fish. Although one hardy fisherman in a dory off Cape Ann took a shot at the monster and swears he hit it and other mariners have pursued the serpent, no specimen has ever been brought ashore. In the 19th century a New Bedford whaler in the Pacific was said to have killed one and the crew hoisted his head and skeleton aboard. The whaler was later lost with all hands in the Arctic and with it the only tangible evidence of the existence of a sea serpent. The story comes to us from the crew of a nearby ship. The number of credible witnesses who have stated under oath they have seen the creature off the Yankee Coast are too impressive to be ignored, but folks ashore have made life miserable for them by numerous intimations that they were either drunk or mentally unbalanced at the time or that they stand in grave need of a visit to the oculist. So the sea serpent remains in a sort of legendary shadowland; even more so than the Vermont Panther, who, years ago on a few occasions was incautious enough to let himself get caught and stuffed.

SEA TURN

A breeze off the water anywhere along the Yankee Coast. In summer it means relief from a baking hot spell, in winter a relaxation of a cold wave that has rolled down on us out of the Arctic Circle. We have them in Spring and Fall, too; foggy days with a salt smell when it is thick outside and one hears the horn on the lighthouse thuttering away at regular intervals, a steamer whistling somewhere out beyond the ledges and it seems mighty good to be ashore.

SEAT OF WORK

Before he sat down at his little work bench, the old time shoemaker piled up around his seat the leather stock for the number of pairs he planned to do at that sitting. This "seat of work" might take a day, or less, if he had it in mind to hoe his corn or pick some apples or kill a rooster after he got done in his shoeshop. Old timers used the expression "to take a seat of work out on him" to mean a thorough criticism of someone, with every piled up grievance getting the full treatment. Sometimes the critics was to the man's face, but more often not.

SHAVING MUG

In the old days shaving with a straight edge razor required somewhat the skill of a surgeon and was preceded by considerable preparation. A round thin cake of a very latherable soap was placed in the bottom of a mug, moistened and then some vigorous work with the brush produced vast quantities of suds which were at once applied to the patient's face. Then he stropped his razor on a leather strap and commenced to shave with the long, keen blade, taking great pains to keep the nicks on his face down to a minimum and carefully avoiding the jugular vein. When he was done, he applied alum to the bleeding places and went down to his breakfast table. This tiresome and dangerous routine was avoided by many who let the barber do it every morning. Considerable style surrounded this rite in the barber shop, including individual mugs for regular customers. Some high class shops numbered each man's mug in gold figures, so the customer need not suffer the indignity of being lathered from a receptacle used by another. Others had pictures on the mugs to differentiate them; an ice wagon for the man who

149

owned the ice company, a steamer for the fire chief, a book for the lawyer and a red cross for the doctor. Museums furnish us with no device marking the mug of the town's undertaker. Science has swept all this away. Safety and electric razors and chemistry's triumph in producing good latherable soap in tubes has reduced shaving to an easy do it yourself operation. So the barber's one hundred mugs with their distinctive designs have come down off his shelves to become collector's items and his work today consists mainly of haircuts.

SHEET ANCHOR TO WINDWARD

Anything laid by to have at hand in a future emergency. A man who builds up his savings account, carries an extra spare tire on his motor trip, or installs a couple of fire extinguishers in his home is likely to refer to these precautions as a "sheet anchor to windward." This is an old salt's metaphor, going back to the days of sail. If a ship was near a coast and the wind shifted so as to carry her toward the shore, she stood in immediate danger of shipwreck unless she could beat to windward and work out to sea. This was called "making an offing," and it required both good luck and fine seamanship to tack a ship into the teeth of the gale. If a mariner could not "claw off a lee shore," as this maneuver was termed, the next best move was to drop the sheet anchor to windward. This was his heaviest and best anchor; carried amidships. If it held, he was saved from being blown onto a lee shore, which is the worst danger a sailor can face. If he had no sheet anchor to put out to windward, or if it dragged, his vessel would drive ashore, strike, break up, and lucky would any man be who could make the land through the surf pounding over the cruel rocks.

SIDE BAR CUTTER

In the old days, after a heavy snow, the horse on a one horse sleigh on a little traveled up country road had a hard time of it unless his driver had a side bar rig. With this arrangement, the shafts were attached to the right front of the sleigh instead of in the center so the horse could plod along in the rut made by the runners of the sleighs that had gone over the road before him. If the shafts had been in the center, he would have had to wallow along in deep snow until the traffic of several days had beaten down a path and in February there often is not that much of an interval between blizzards. Of course, this problem did not exist on the main highways of the town, for the snow roller and its dozen oxen broke out the road and made a good driving surface. It was on the little used hill roads where the snow roller did not go that the side bar cutter was at a premium. With this rig the horse came up the long grade, without puffing, in the rut where others had gone before. He turned into the barnyard, tail up and with head held high, and did not need to be walked up and down to cool off before being led to

151

his stall. Today the horses are gone, the sleigh is somebody's curio, the big motor plows are out before the snow has stopped falling and if a man cannot drive his automobile to the store without getting out now and then to shovel, the Selectmen hear about it in jig time.

SIDEWHEELER

In the early days of the century, coastal and river steamers abounded, mostly craft with great boxes amidships gaily painted and decorated with scrollwork, the vessel's name and perhaps a picture. Inside the boxes churned the paddle wheels, driving the ship ahead with a commotion of splashing and foaming that was really something to see. The boat to Portland or Bangor or New York or Lubec or Hartford or Yarmouth was ready to give us a short experience of the mystery of the sea; the landmarks of the harbor and shore slowly fading astern, the rush of water along the hull, then the pitch and roll of the ocean swell, sunset across the waters, flashing lighthouses, at bedtime a bunk where one was rocked to sleep by the motion of the ship, and perhaps if there was a fog, to be awakened in the small hours by the deep voice of our vessel's steam whistle warning others that we were there, and their answering voices coming over the waters, some near, some so far away as to seem like a sound from beyond this world. In the morning any enterprising lad was on deck early, prowling around in the mists of dawn, on the lookout for the first sight of a new harbor, a place he had never seen before, shining brightly before him as the rising sun burned away the overcast and his vessel came steaming grandly up the channel while he surveyed a world that was all his. Progress; super-highways, planes, huge trucks that took away the freight business, have spelled the end of all this.

SITTING BRITCHES

When the old timers said of anyone "He has his sitting britches on," they referred more to a state of mind than an actual garment. Such a person was one in the mood to take his ease and stay and stay and stay, instead of getting on about his business. And a corollary is that he talked and talked in a vein not at all entertaining. Mayhap this expression indicates the impatience of the host as much as the over-inclination of the guest to remain too long on his posterior.

SLEIGHING

"Six weeks sleighing in April" describes one of those mean Spring seasons that is not Spring at all, but a time of disappointment and frustration when Winter frequently revisits those of us who are fools enough to keep on living up this way. Many a man can recall a sleigh ride on Easter Sunday, — bright sunlight, the snow drifts flecked with the red of the fallen husks from bursting maple buds and bare ground under the runners by noontime. In such a season there still are drifts of dirty corn snow along the hill and country roads in the last week of April, nobody can put in his early planting of peas, and even the peepers in the swamps are late getting started.

SLUMGULLION

In the nature of a stew, popular with campers, men whose wives are away, and folks who have not had time to do their shopping. Ingredients: water in a kettle, sliced onion, a meat bone, a can of corn or string beans or tomatoes, a handful of rice, potatoes, the last of a loaf of bread, a piece of a red pepper, anything else which would be thrown away if not used. Old timers say the idea came from the Gypsies, who kept a kettle going over their camp fire at all times, putting into it whatever came to hand, were it a rabbit, a pheasant, a string of trout, a hatful of apples or a box of chowder crackers. Recipes for this dish vary.

SMIDGIN

A small quantity of any substance, but most frequently something used in cookery. This is one of the words the very sound of which suggest its meaning. The schoolmen would say it is an excellent example of onomatopoeia.

SMOKE CLOSET

A small compartment built into the big central chimney of an old fashioned house with apertures at top and bottom to permit the smoke from the fireplace to pass through. In it were kept hams and bacon so that the wood smoke might complete the curing process and keep them in good state of preservation. The smoke closet was well above the fireplace, perhaps at the second floor, so the contents might have the beneficial effect of the smoke without being exposed to too much heat. In the old days there was no mechanical refrigeration, nor had the ice chest, using cakes cut in winter from ponds, been developed to any extent, so any other means of preserving food had to be utilized as fully as possible.

SMOKE HOUSE

A place for curing meat or fish by hanging it in an atmosphere of smoke from a slow wood fire. Ham, bacon and herring are most generally given this treatment. The smoke house is a shed with small spaces between the boards of the side walls and it may be of any size, those in seaport towns where a lot of herring is brought in often being quite large. The fish are hung on long sticks thrust through the gills, the fire not being lighted until the place is full of long rows ready for curing. Just any old wood will not do for a well run smoke house. A careful operator uses hickory, thus imparting a special and superior flavor to his ham or bacon or fish. Smoke is composed of the minute particles of whatever is burning, and these particles deposited on the meat or fish are what preserve it and flavor it. Therefore there is a great difference in the results from a hickory fire and one fueled by the staves of an old tar barrel. Smoking is one of the many processes used since time immemorial for preserving food and it continues in wide use today, in spite of modern refrigeration, because of the flavor it imparts.

SNOW EATER

A sea turn in late February or early March coming in from the south or southeast. The warm air from off the ocean reduces the snow cover as does not even the sunniest day, there is a lot of fog, usually a drizzle of rain, mist rises from the drifts, the water runs at the roadsides, and the brooks are bank full. Here and there, as the snow is eaten away, appear patches of moist grass, and for one who looks sharp, the first faint tint of green.

SNOW ROLLER

A large wooden roller six feet or more high and a little wider than a span of horses. Before motorization and hard roads every north country town had one and after a deep snow four or five yoke of oxen would be hitched up to it and the roads would be rolled so there would be a well packed surface for sleighing. A horse flounders in heavy snow and drifts but the solidly built oxen breast through the meanest going, taking their time about it, yet never letting up. As the use of automobiles increased, people wanted bare roads, not a highway well covered with the packed down snow that makes such good sleighing. So today the big motor plows push the snow to the roadsides, scraping down to the macadam surface, and the old snow rollers stand out back of the town hall, rotting away.

SNOW TRAIN

A Yankee plan devised in the darkest days of the Depression of the early Thirties to get some cash money from Northern New England's never failing crop of snow. The architect of this scheme was the Boston & Maine Railroad; the ingredients a Mogul locomotive, three wooden "open ender" coaches, and a few dozen placards posted in the North Station and stations in the suburban area. When nine o'clock on Sunday morning arrived the skiers were there in numbers, a couple of cars were hurriedly added and

157

the first Snow Train chugged out through the North Station yards, loaded to the gunwales and headed for the hills of New Hampshire. At an up country station the Snow Train went onto a siding, the skiers piled out, every slope and field was soon crisscrossed with ski tracks, amateurs took spills and the more expert showed off. The village store sold out of everything edible, so did the sandwich man, the natives marvelled as they watched and scurried around making more sandwiches and the city folks had a whale of a time. When the winter sun was low over the hills the Mogul locomotive blew long blasts to get everyone aboard and started back to Boston with its cars of tired, red-cheeked passengers, singing and chattering. Next morning, when the Railroad's accounting department had cast up its figures, officials rushed the printing of placards for another Snow Train.

SORTER'S THUMB

A term common in the tanner's trade, referring to the sensitivity of touch of the man who grades hides. Facing a big heap of skins, he can sort them out into different piles according to their quality, relying somewhat on their appearance, yet much more on the feel of them. The boss does not set any Tom, Dick or Harry to this job, but only a man who has demonstrated the judgment to separate the skins accurately and quickly. A tannery is a good place to make money and an easy place to lose it. Selling good skins with a lot of inferior ones is wasteful and letting a few poor hides go out with a shipment of high priced merchandise angers good customers. So the man with the sorter's thumb has always been well paid in the tanneries since colonial days, and if he slips out for a drink nothing is ever said unless he has so many that his sense of touch is impaired.

SORTILEGE

Old time Yankees sought help in time of trouble by laying the Bible flat on the table in the "front room," thrusting in a finger at random and opening "the Good Book" at that point. Every verse on the two open pages was then studied with infinite care to see if in one of them lay the answer to the problem and generally they found that some one in Biblical days had travelled the same rough road and managed to get over it somehow.

STADDLE

A circle of short heavy stakes driven into the surface of a salt marsh to support a hay cock above the level of an unusually high tide, for salt hay is usually stacked on the marsh until needed. Staddles are to be seen today in many salt marshes along our coast; some are relics of a past when salt hay was important to the owners of herds of cows long since vanished; some are still in active use in areas where dairying continues to be a large factor in the eco-

nomic life of the community. In the Newbury and Rowley Marsh region of the Parker River the staddles, topped by symmetrically shaped haystacks, are a picturesque subject for artists and photographers.

STEAMER PORTLAND

The most talked of vessel in the entire history of New England shipping, this comfortable old sidewheeler left India Wharf, Boston, at 7 p.m. on November 26, 1898 and headed down the harbor, Portland bound, into the teeth of one of the fiercest blizzards ever to ravage the Yankee coast. The glow of her lights, the majestic up and down motion of her walking beam soon faded from sight in the swirling wall of snow. Those on the pier turned to go home, shaking their heads and wondering how

160

the vessel would fare once she was beyond Graves Light and the thunderous waves of the North Atlantic storm commenced to strike her under her overhang. They were the last to see the PORTLAND as a ship, although over the years various people have claimed they saw her off Thatcher's Island and at various other points. And those folks on India Wharf were the last to see any of her 176 people alive. Somewhere on her northeastward course, probably before she cleared Cape Ann, the brute fury of the Atlantic was too much for her. Did Captain Blanchard come about and run before the gale? Did he lose his bearings or was he blown off his course; what were those last hours aboard the PORTLAND like? No one knows; we can only guess, for all aboard were lost and in the morning the steamer's wreckage lay strewn along the beaches of Cape Cod near Peaked Hill Bars and Highland Light. And some of the bodies were there too, cast onto the sands by the pounding surf as the sun broke through the clouds on a raging sea and a land deep in snow drifts. Stateroom doors, oars, the saloon's red plush furniture, one of the big paddle wheels came ashore, but her hull lay out there somewhere in Davy Jones locker, and many of her passengers and crew with her. Yankees have never forgotten the ship and to this day, when the wind howls and the roar of the breakers is heard well away from the shore and the snow stings a man's face so he hurries for shelter, they say "It's like the night the Portland went down."

STEAM FIRE ENGINE

From the mid-Nineteenth Century until after World War I the mainstay of American fire departments. Gradually replacing the old "hand tub" in the days before the Civil War, it, in its turn, was supplanted by the motor fire engine. The "steamer" had a vertical steam boiler, generally a piston pump, an air dome to equalize pressure and the larger ones delivered up to 1000 gallons a minute. Hot water was maintained in the boiler at all times by a connection to a heater in the cellar of the fire station. When the alarm struck, the steamer's three horses galloped from the stalls to take their places under the harnesses suspended by cords from the ceiling, the driver lowered this "quick hitch" onto the horses, snapped the collars, leaped to his seat and was away. Mean-

162

while the stoker flipped a lever that closed off the connection with the hot water heater in the cellar and touched a match to the two bushels of excelsior and kindling wood in the steamer's firebox. Down the street the heavy machine rumbled, following the hose-wagon, black smoke and sparks pouring from its stack, bell ringing, horses galloping; one of the most picturesque sights of its day. And pumping at a fire it was even more to watch; — with cannel coal as fuel it punched a straight column of smoke thirty feet high, it jumped up and down on its carriage with the motion of the piston strokes, nickelled rods flashed, the fly wheel spun, red hot coals flecked its black smoke. The stoker poked and shoveled and whistled for the fuel wagon. The engineer, his horses unhitched and in a place of safety, walked around his machine with an oil can, watching his pressure guages. The motor pump delivers as good a stream, is faster, lighter, requires but one operator, and throws no sparks to set fire to nearby roofs. The steamer, obsolete, is now a museum piece, but there are plenty of old timers who would go on a day's journey to see one in action once more.

STIVVER

To get moving. A mother would say to her boy, "Now stivver along to the store and don't be all day about it." Sometimes it was used to describe hard going. An old lady might sigh and say, "Well, I'll manage to stivver along somehow."

163

STONE SLOOP

A small sailing craft engaged in transporting granite paving blocks, curbstones and building trim from the quarries at Rockport on Cape Ann to Boston and New York. Water transportation of bulky cargo is always cheaper, so many of these workhorse vessels mogged along the coast carrying Rockport's famous granite to pave the streets and construct the buildings of the large cities. Skipper and crew led a leisurely life with plenty of time for contemplation and reading on these slow moving ships. However, they had to look sharp when any kind of sea kicked up, for if the timbers got to working and a couple of seams opened up, it did not do to try too valiantly to keep ahead of the leak with the pumps. A cargo of granite can go to Davy Jones locker with great swiftness, so they kept the boats slung outboard and if their sloop commenced to settle, they abandoned ship on the run. These craft always steered a course near the shore so the crew would not have too long a row if the weight of the cargo and the pounding of the waves proved too much for the vessel to survive. When the use of granite in buildings and for paving blocks declined, this coastal trade became a thing of the past.

SUCCOTASH

A tasty dish of hulled corn, shell beans, some milk and seasoned to suit the cook. It makes a meal that stays with a man and is a main course if one is hard up, or far from a store, or a blizzard is raging outside and supplies are a mite short. The Indians gave us succotash. Made from their two principal crops, corn and beans, it was easy to carry on the march and could be cooked up in no time in an iron kettle over a wood fire.

SUGAR LOAF

In the old days sugar came in the form of a symmetrical cone shaped loaf from which small pieces were cut as needed. Only upon unusual occasions did the lady of the house go to her sugar loaf, which was kept carefully wrapped in paper in a dry place such as the little closets set into the big chimney. The art of sugar making has progressed steadily so that sugar is now much cheaper than in the old days, and therefore a common household article. The name "Sugar Loaf" is sometimes applied to a hill or mountain of symmetrical contour.

SULPHUR AND MOLASSES

A concoction composed of these two ingredients and none other, combined in such proportions as one's mother, or sometimes grandmother, in her infinite wisdom deemed best. Thought to be the sovereign remedy for the most common of non-contagious diseases, Spring Fever, it was administered regularly in most old time households at about the time of the

Vernal Equinox. The children were lined up and
made to take it, and no back talk, if you please. The
lassitude accompanying Spring Fever was promptly
eliminated, the children quickly became more active
and by the time this rugged medicine's job was done,
the youngsters had a new outlook on life. Modern
medicine has given us new remedies for Spring
Fever, as for everything else, that doubtless do the
work much better and with infinitely less commotion,
yet Sulphur and Molasses still remains as one of the
things a real New Englander thinks of as a part of
Spring, along with dandelions and the first robin,
marbles and baseball games, an occasional fine day
and the sound of the peepers in the swamps on a
warm evening.

SUPPER FIRE

In the old days when Meal No. 3 was not dinner, but supper, a housewife commenced her preparations by building a fire of small dry sticks in her kitchen stove. Then she set about getting ready whatever she was going to cook, pausing from time to time to put another stick in the stove. Running a supper fire is an art now familiar to few, for today the lady of the house need do no more than turn on her gas stove. A well run wood fire gave a quick and intense heat; in the hands of an expert every bit as good as gas. Toward day's end columns of blue smoke rose from the chimneys of the town and one homeward bound might catch the sweet pungent smell of the burning wood.

SWALLOW THE ANCHOR

To give up seafaring and find a job ashore. In the early 1800s in prosperous seaport towns like Salem and Portsmouth and Newburyport, people said "he has come ashore for good" to mean that a man had made enough money from his share as a ship's officer so that he could set himself up as a merchant or ship chandler or perhaps establish a rope walk. Most men went to sea because there lay opportunity and when success came, they were happy to think they no longer had to face the North Atlantic in winter or risk the typhoons of the China Sea and the pirates of the Malay archipelago. Sailors always talk of a farm ashore, or a shop. Yet many an old time mariner tired of the smell of the land some morning was down at the waterfront, longing to see blue water once again and ready to sign aboard.

SWAN BOATS

One of the outstanding features of Boston's famous Public Garden. Each boat consists of two pontoons upon which are mounted a half dozen seats of the park bench type and at the stern an enormous metal representation of a swan, gleaming white and hollow, inside of which sits the man who makes the thing go. Usually a young fellow earning his way through college, he works a bicycle contraption that powers a small paddle wheel and with ropes attached to a rudder he steers the craft. At a small pier at the Charles Street side of the Public Garden's pond he takes aboard his passengers; small children escorted by parents, high school kids visiting Boston, sailors on shore leave, tourists, and generally one or two folks with gray in their hair who can remember when mother took them on this very same voyage. Around the pond they go, under the beautiful bridge, by the big bronze Japanese lantern, moving slowly past the well kept flower beds along the shore and the ducks feeding in the shallows. The half dozen swan boats have been navigating these waters since 1877, all that time under the management of the Paget family, without ever a claim being presented to the Marine insurance company that covers them.

Unless one has circumnavigated the pond on one of these vessels, he has not really seen Boston.

SWITCHEL

A temperance drink for haying time; its ingredients cold spring water, molasses and ginger. To be any good at all it had to be poured into a large earthern jug and left in the shade of the big elm tree over at the side of the field, well covered with leaves and grass or a damp gunny sack. In the days when all the mowing was done by men with scythes, haying was mighty hot work and the only relief was a trip over to the switchel jug and a few gurgles of the tart drink. Sometimes it was spiked with a good jorum or two of rum, although that was a risky business when a half dozen haying hands were swinging along together with their scythes, for some half jingled fellow might get out of rhythm and take a mean nick from the leg of the man ahead of him.

SYMPTOM BOOK

No master of an old square rigger would have thought of going to sea without his symptom book, for not only was he captain and the ship's clergyman, but its physician as well. This volume described in detail the manifestations of each ailment so the skipper might diagnose Jack Tar's illness and complete directions for treatment were included. With some books came a small chest of medicines, each

169

bottle being numbered, and for each illness a dose from one of the numbered bottles was prescribed. The difficulty with this system is best illustrated by the sea captain who, after examining the patient and coming to a decision as to what his disease was, read on and found that it called for a dose from Bottle No. 8. It turned out that No. 8 was empty, so since two fours are eight, and always have been, he gave the man a double dose from Bottle No. 4. Although the patient lived, his unhappy condition for a couple of days convinced the captain that in this instance mathematical logic had failed. Fortunately infections on ship board were rare because salt water, one of the finest disinfectants, was always applied at once if a man was cut. For the setting of a broken bone, the anesthesia was rum and lots of it, and then, two shipmates sat on the patient, the mate read the directions from the book, and the captain went to work setting and splinting. For the extraction of a tooth, he had an instrument, gory but effective, and the sailor's woes, very real, were finally drowned in rum and he was allowed to stay below for a couple of watches.

TAPEWORM

 To one with a large appetite old timers would say "You must have a tapeworm" and this was generally good for a laugh. The actuality was no joke, a parasite in the human intestine sometimes attaining a length as great as 15 ft. Not unusual in the days before rigid inspection of meat, it originated with the worm's egg in beef and grew upon entering a human body. The remedy was a day of fasting, then a jorum of strong physic and after that a nurse or doctor or a member of the family stood by with a handful of snap clothes pins. When the creature first appeared at the patient's nether orifice, a clothes pin was snapped on him least he retreat. With skillful manipulation, a cooperative patient and plenty of luck the tapeworm was sometimes removed whole. In that event the proud owner might place it in a glass jar of alcohol and exhibit it in the window of the local drugstore to be viewed by everyone interested in the marvels of nature.

TAUT SHIP

When all the standing rigging was tightened so each stay and shroud was like a bow string; when the running rigging showed no slack anywhere and was neatly belayed, with the ends of every brace and sheet and halyard flemished down in a neat coil; when the woodwork was always painted, the brightwork shone like an African's eye, the deck planking holystoned white, and no sailor dared to spit to windward or wear a dirty shirt on Sunday, that skipper was said to be master of "a taut ship." Mariners described the other kind as "a slack ship." The life of jar tar aboard a taut ship was likely to be an arduous one, always busy during his watch on deck, with little chance to stand in the lee of the galley, light a pipe and swap yarns. Although he was generally so tired he was glad to climb into his bunk to snatch forty winks on his watch below, the sailor aboard a windjammer preferred a taut ship to a slack one, for he trusted such a skipper in a howling gale or in waters where an iceberg might loom up in the fog, and he figured the old man would make a hot fight of it if a pirate craft put out from some tropical inlet, her bulwarks lined with murderous picaroons. In the old navy Commodore Preble commanded a taut ship and a taut squadron. His men cursed him in several languages when the rope's end curled around their ribs, yet he led them to victory over the Bashaw of Tripoli and they knew they served under a great man.

THICK OF SNOW

The mariner's term for a snow fall with big, wet flakes and plenty of them, blowing and swirling so visibility ahead is nearly zero, and a good sailor heaves to or drops anchor. This condition might occur during a blizzard, although it is more likely to exist in a shorter storm, when the flakes are larger than the cold, hard, wind-driven snow the north-easter hits us with. The day after such a storm, folks ashore exclaim at the beauty of the trees with their every branch and twig gleaming white in the sun, but the old salt may be telling about the schooner that "piled up on Outer Ledge in that thick o' snow."

THROW A TUB TO THE WHALE

To give in to anyone, to let him have his way. An old Nantucket and New Bedford expression having rise in the technique of whaling. When the boat neared the whale, the harpooner made his cast, sinking the weapon deep in the body of the leviathan. Then the battle began and the whale, who had a few tricks of his own, might race across the ocean waters at such speed that the boat might put bows under and be swamped. Or the whale might "sound," going far down into the ocean deeps. In either case the boatmen paid out the line attached to the harpoon, a line coiled in a tub amidships. If, after all the line in the tub was paid out, the whale was still traveling at such speed that the boat was in danger of being swamped, or if the monster had gone so deep and the line was all out and the boat was likely to be pulled under, the tub was thrown overboard and the whale won out, making off with harpoon, line, tub and all. Slowly the men rowed back to the ship to report that they "threw the tub to the whale." The captain generally understood, for he knew they were fighting the world's biggest living creature, an animal beside which the dragons of mythology were but puny things. Sea language comes ashore, so today the expression is used to denote the act of giving in. Even when a baby sitter on Nantucket has to give in to an obstreperous brat, she may sigh and say, "I'm going to throw the tub to the whale."

TIDE MILL

Near the coast where the land is flat and no brook or river has enough of a drop to turn a water wheel, the old timers relied on the tide for power to run their grist mills. When the incoming tide had filled whatever reservoir they were able to build, the gates in the dam were closed and at ebb tide the water ran down a sluiceway to turn the water wheel. Since the mill could be run only at ebb tide and in the early stages of flood tide, it was often necessary to work by night if the grist was to be ground. A man who had a mill inland, with a constant supply of water behind a dam, fed by a brook or river, could keep gentleman's hours. Tide mills ground not only the farmer's grain, but as foreign trade grew and Yankee ships brought in tropical products, they did a brisk business grinding coffee, pepper, chocolate and spices. Revere, East Saugus and Kennebunkport were the sites of well known tide mills until fairly recent times. Today any one wishing power to run a small manufactory telephones the local electric utility, a cable is run into his premises, and he is ready to start his machines. The tide mill was developed in a day when there was no electric power, coal was little known and the art of metal working was so primitive that even wood burning steam boilers had not been developed. The miller used a wooden water wheel, wooden shaft, usually wooden gears and cheerfully performed the labor of building a dam so he could get into business.

TIGHTER

Over the ages people have said "tighter than a drum" or "tighter than the bark on a tree." Some Yankees with a love for the more graphic said 'tighter than a bull's mouth in fly time" and his contemporaries, adopting the expression, used it with such frequency that it has come down to us. To appreciate it, one must have experienced the assaults of black flies in the country in first warm weather and the depredations of horse flies in the late summer, whose bite draws blood. The bull, to avoid extreme discomfort, must see to it that any body aperture is kept tightly closed lest one or more of these pestiferous insects enter and make him miserable in that part of his anatomy.

TILLER MAN

The fire department's aerial ladder truck, by far the longest vehicle on the road, requires a steersman for the rear as well as the front wheels. Were he not perched up there way aft of the driver, it would be impossible to get the truck around ordinary street corners without slowing to a crawl. Even at a slow pace the end of the "big stick," which projects a dozen feet beyond the rear wheels, might slam into an elm tree or poke the glass out of a store window. The tiller man solves it all; at the rear steering wheel he guides the after part of the truck through the traffic, sweeps it around corners in a graceful and accurate curve and at the fire he hops down and goes to work with the rest of the company. A man of nerve and judgment and rugged physique, he is one of the romantic figures left in today's scene, doing his spectacular task with all the verve and dash of a cowboy or a cavalryman.

TO HELL I PITCH IT

One of the expressions that marks a Marbleheader, be he walking along Front Street down by the harbor or serving aboard a U. S. cruiser on the Mediterranean station. Lobstermen say it, and so do schoolboys and respectable ladies and men who set out in the morning for their jobs in fancy offices up in Boston. Tell a Marbleheader that it is profane and he, or she, will look at you in amazement and ask you what in hell you mean.

TOWN BULL

One maintained by the town by a tax levied on each cow. In colonial times the selectmen named a committee to procure bulls, decide where they should be

kept so each part of the town would have good service, who should care for them, how much the compensation was to be and whether a particular bull should go at large or be confined. They had the further power to prosecute anyone when he did not do his part. That bulls were so scarce as to require governmental action to provide them was due to economic reasons. Young bulls either became veal early in life or underwent a change that made them oxen, — peaceful and very useful draft animals. A bull allowed to reach unaltered maturity was a difficult character; so ugly he might attack anyone at any time, useless as a draft animal because no man could compel him to submit to the yoke, and in his old age valuable only for sausage. But without him there would be no more calves. So the Bull Committee stepped in, clothed with the authority of law, collected taxes and paid one farmer in each district to keep one of the ornery critters. The supply of milk, butter, cheese, beef, and oxen for draft animals all depended upon seeing to it that a "good" bull was never too distant, so the townspeople, in meeting assembled,

177

cheerfully voted the cow tax as readily as they appropriated money for the schoolmaster's and the minister's pay.

TRAVELING SALESMAN

A rugged man in the days before automobiles came into general use, who horsed his sample cases and his valises in and out of railroad trains, stage coaches, buckboards and country hotels. He really covered the country stores, showed his customers everything, took his time and put in long hours roosting around at junctions waiting for the up train or the down train or the branch local. With a big black cigar, a celluloid collar and an infinite fund of patience, odd bits of news and funny stories, he was a friendly fellow, eagerly awaited by the folks along his route. Sometimes he hired a buggy to drive himself and his samples to towns not accessible by rail and he might be several days clopping along the old dirt roads, calling at village stores and putting up at farmhouses if no hotel was near at sundown. So it was that the traveling salesman became a legendary figure, celebrated in song and story and in every one of these romantic ballads and racy anecdotes the part of the female lead is played by the farmer's daughter. Today his work is done by a man in a motor car who has a clean shirt every day, gets his business done with dispatch and, if he is away over night, probably telephones his wife long distance and then goes to the movies.

TRIM WATCH

The task of one or two of the crew of a sidewheel steamer who were charged with the duty of rolling lead weighted barrels from one side to the other of the freight deck to keep the vessel on an even keel. These boats, coming down from Boston and making several stops at points along the Kennebec or the Penobscot, had high super-structures and the wind would give them a list to port or starboard. When the indicator in the pilot house showed a list, the man at the wheel rang a bell that sounded on the freight deck, the number of blows signifying how many of the 800 pound barrels he wanted moved and to which side of the ship. To have the steamer level, or on "an even keel" was important so that each of the paddle wheels would do its share of the work and take the same "bite" of water. These boats, the "City of Bangor," the "City of Rockland," the "Ransom B. Fuller" and the others gave the small coastal and river ports freight and passenger service that was quicker and cheaper than anything the railroads could offer. As for a trip over the road, such a thing was almost unheard of in the early part of the century. Leaving Boston at 5 p.m., the passenger would eat a luxurious dinner as the boat steamed out past the islands of Boston harbor and turned east, leaving Nahant to port. By the time the vessel was off Thatcher's Island he could walk the deck for a while, watching the lights along the shore and the majestic motion of the walking beam and then to bed for a solid sleep, so as to be up early to get off at Bucksport or Rockport or Castine. Sometimes a morning fog shut down like a thick blanket and the pilot worked his way up river, whistling so he could tell where he was by the way the sound echoed back from the hills along shore. These boats are gone, their work now done by modern motor vehicles roaring over superhighways.

TROUT IN THE WELL

A careful householder often caught a trout and dropped him in the well so the fish would keep the water clean by eating insects, larvae and green algae. Most people in the country felt that water a trout could live in was bound to be good, pure drinking water. Although some folks, instead of a well, had spring water piped into a cistern made of a half hogshead and setting beside the kitchen sink, yet they kept a trout swimming around in their drinking water as a guarantee of purity. The fish grew as time went on, but he never lived long enough to outgrow the well or cistern, for boys loved to dangle a baited hook before the trout's nose when no one was looking, snatch him out and have him pan fried for breakfast. When this happened the head of the house set out for the brook that came down off the hillside, and generally he knew of a pool where he could catch another trout without being too long about it.

180

TURTLE FEAST

The story begins about the year 1800 with a West India Turtle unfortunate enough to be captured by some natives while dozing in the sun on a sand bar. Flipping him onto his back, the natives manhandled the monster, over 4 feet long and a yard wide, into their dug-out canoe and headed for port. At Havana or Port au Prince or Kingston, or whatever harbor they put into, they looked for a Salem shipmaster willing to pay in silver coin. The turtle headed North, still on his back, his destiny now certain, and when the vessel made Salem the word was quickly passed around town that the Marine Society or the House of Derby or the Crowninshields or the Forresters, or perhaps Billy Gray, would have a Turtle Feast near a sandy beach somewhere in Salem Bay, perhaps on one of the islands. Done in the grand manner, this sumptuous meal was prepared by Prince Hall of Boston, a tall and dignified negro who came down with his staff of helpers whenever Salem's wealthy merchants put on something extra special. A big tent was pitched, the turtle was cooked in a huge iron pot over a roaring driftwood fire, the fixings were prepared by the helpers at tables nearby and at last an enormous Turtle Pie, served in the creature's shell, was brought into the tent, borne on the shoulders of four of Prince Hall's black men. The guests, mostly sea captains and merchants, ate and swapped yarns about every sea and bay and river and inlet on the face of the globe and drank

Madeira wine aged by travelling twice around the Cape of Good Hope in the hold of a Salem ship and in the gloaming they sailed back to town, — full.

TWO LAMPS BURNING AND NO SHIP AT SEA

An expression used by folks in the ports along the Yankee Coast to signify wastefulness and improvidence. In the old days a lamp to provide light was considerable of an advance over candles or a burning pine knot. It was a luxury; expensive because it required the purchase of whale oil, whereas candles and pitchy pieces of pine were produced on the place. Therefore a person who not only spent cash to purchase whale oil at the store, but then had two lamps burning when one is enough for ordinary folks was deemed very extravagant. Unless, and this is important, unless he had a ship at sea, therefore being one of the merchant class reasonably expecting profits from a cargo, advantageously traded for by his captain in some far away place such as Zanzibar or Canton or Naples or St. Eustatia. For anyone without expectations from a ship at sea to indulge in any such vainglorious illumination was, the old timers felt, extravagance enough to indicate the man was "just a plain fool."

UNICORN

A critter appearing in the fables of antiquity, resembling a horse, and with a single horn issuing from his forehead. The unicorn "supports" one side of the British coat of arms, the lion the other, so one was placed on the east facade of the Old State House in Boston when it was built in 1713, and also a lion, to show that this was the headquarters of English power. When the Declaration of Independence was first read from the balcony, July 18, 1776, the exuberant mob promptly ripped off the lion and the unicorn and burned them in the middle of State Street to signalize the end of the King's dominion over Massachusetts. In 1881, when the building was restored, a new unicorn and lion were mounted on the east facade. Done over in metal, they are there today, looking across 3,000 miles of ocean toward Old England. On the opposite end is mounted the American eagle, wings spread, and he faces west, from his eminence surveying 3,000 miles of his own country.

VAMP IT UP

The vamp is the upper part of a shoe, and this expression is used in the shoe-making towns to mean strengthen, patch, or provide with a new part. The modern colloquialism "beef it up" has the same meaning. "Vamp it up" is not to be confused with the verb "to vamp" common in the Roaring Twenties, frequently applied to seductive behavior by the female of the species. The more recent verb is derived from the fancy that a too enterprising woman resembles the aggressive vampire bat in pursuit of its victim.

VERMONT PANTHER

The animal which the wiseacres say does not exist today except in the minds of fearful people who imagine things on a dark night. However, it did exist, for a dozen husky specimens have been killed in the state, the most notable being the Wardsboro panther of 1875 and the Barnard panther of 1881. In appearance a panther might look like a western mountain lion or cougar, although the Barnard panther looks more like a huge house cat with enormous hind quarters, a short tail and perhaps could be termed a "catamount." He is stuffed and on exhibition in the State House at Montpelier. Although since 1881 no one has bagged a panther in Vermont, many claim to have seen one, footprints of a predatory animal much larger than a lynx have been found in various parts of the state, livestock has been killed in a manner suggesting a fierce and heavy assailant and in the back hills the characteristic blood curdling cry has been heard at night. As late as 1932 a panther was shot in New Brunswick, so it is not unlikely that they exist in Vermont, since the state's forest areas have increased as trees grow up on the abandoned hill farms and the deer population, upon which these big cats thrive, is on the increase. Reports of their presence continue to be received occasionally and experienced naturalists think that some day a hunter in one of our three northern states will come in with a panther. When he does, he will have headlines in the Boston papers. The old timers had various names for the critter, such as catamount, Indian devil, painter, or "the varmint."

VISITING FIREMAN

Anyone who drops in for a call upon a fellow in his trade or profession in another town, be he a banker, a plumber, an engineer or a mortician. If he finds that some feature of his business is better done where he is visiting, he observes and learns and carries new knowledge home with him. If, as is more likely the case, he discovers that these people are a bit behind the game, he instructs them in the more advanced methods and equipment he uses in his work, and begrudges none of the time spent bringing enlightenment to his hosts. Applied now to anyone who likes to see how his opposite number in another town does things, the term originated in the fireman's unfailing attraction to the nearest fire station when away from home. Truly called to his profession, he examines with an expert eye the other town's apparatus, swaps yarns about tough fires and if the tapper hits, he is on the rear step when the engine swings out of the house. If it is a working fire, he borrows helmet, coat and boots and pitches in with the rest of them, for he is bound that no one shall ever call him a "sidewalk fireman." When the fire is out, he rides back to the house on the kit, dirty and happy, washes up with the company and goes his way, the richer by another experience and another story to tell when he gets back to his own outfit.

THE WAGON

 (A) a light truck with an enclosed body, open at the back, with a rear step and grab handles and narrow wooden benches along both sides, used by police to transport prisoners from the place of arrest to the local lockup. Few remember the days when the police used a horse drawn vehicle for this purpose, yet the cops and everyone else generally refer to the modern equipage as "the wagon." Sometimes it is termed the "Black Maria" on account of its color and the ominous nature of its mission and occasionally the "paddy wagon," this last expression referring to the racial origin of those who operate it. It is used frequently to remove the ill or the injured to the hospital, it then being called not "the wagon," but "the ambulance." (B) On the wagon; total abstention from intoxicating liquor after a long history of over-indulgence. This state of continued sobriety is occasionally permanent, but more often temporary. The metaphor in full is "on the water wagon," a wholly mythical vehicle.

WALKING BEAM

Along the shores of New England harbors and rivers there was a lot to watch in the days when every town big enough to be a dot on the map was a port of call for a steamboat of some sort. They were mostly paddle wheel craft and no boy who loved to watch what was going on will forget all the foaming and splashing as the blades bit the water and the vessel came up to the pier. Atop the uppermost deck house, the walking beam, on a vertical upright and pinioned in its exact center, moved majestically up and down as the long rod from the steam engine pushed one end up and the rod on the other end reached down to the crank on the shaft between the two paddle wheels. This is the most primitive application of steam power; a steam cylinder pushing a rod that moves one end of a balanced lever while the other end of the lever is connected to a rotating shaft. For many years this was the only method available to drive steamships, even those in trans-Atlantic service. Gradually the development of the triple expansion engine and the propellor supplanted the paddle wheel vessels; there was less to see, yet such vessels were safer in a rough sea since there were no huge over-hanging paddle boxes to be ripped off by the angry waves. The engines of a propellor driven craft were well worth sneaking into a forbidden part of a ship to watch; a study for any thoughtful lad, for, as Kipling said in *MacAndrew's* Hymn, they demonstrate "interdependence absolute, foreseen, ordained, decreed." Today we have steam turbines and diesels; they hum busily and do a superb job, yet the romance of action and movement is no longer there.

WARM FROM THE COW

In these times of refrigeration, pasteurization and urban living there are few children who have ever had a drink of milk "warm from the cow." In the old times the kids hung around the barn in the late afternoon and if they were real good, did not distract the cows and stood well with whoever was doing the milking, they got a drink right then and there. In it were all the micro-organisms that frequent barns and ride around on cows, and a modern parent would be horrified, but the children loved it and most of them managed to survive.

WARMING PAN

A round brass receptacle about a foot in diameter having a tight fitting hinged cover pierced with small holes and decorated with filligree work, and a long wooden handle artfully turned from a piece of choice wood. The old timers kept their warming pans near the big fireplace in the living room and on a cold winter night, just before they banked the fire, a shovelfull of glowing coals was placed in the pan and the cover securely fastened. Up in the bedroom the warming pan was thrust between the ice cold sheets, moved around a bit and then left in one desired spot until undressing was speedily accomplished. Then out from the bed came the warming pan, in went Mr. and Mrs. and human bodies took over the project of keeping the bed warm. In those days central heating with a register or radiator in each room was unheard of, so a bedroom was generally nearly as cold as outdoors. Although the mansions of the wealthy had fireplaces in the bedrooms that served to take off some of the chill, it was still mighty helpful to have the warming pans between the icy sheets in the winter months. A much told story has it that a Yankee skipper discovered on reaching Havana that he had a few cases of warming pans included by mistake in his cargo. However, he did not carry them back to Boston with him. He persuaded some of the sugar planters that these were ideal molasses ladles and he made a good profit on the transaction.

A warming pan is a choice antique today, but be sure it has a good handle before you pay much for it.

WASHSTAND

A small square table in the upper left shelf of which was cut a circular hole of the size to receive the lower part of a large crockery washbasin and hold it firm no matter how much the user sloshed his sponge or wash cloth around in it. Around this top ran a rim a few inches high to protect the wall paper from splashings and on the rim was a small shelf for toilet articles. The lower level of the washstand provided space for soap, liniment, sponge, hair oil, bay rum, and brush and comb and on the sides were towel racks. Below was a small drawer for medicines and extra soap. With a crockery pitcher full of water standing in the bowl, a slop jar beside the washstand and a vessel under the bed, one had a complete bathroom right in the bedroom. This arrangement required more work than the modern masterpiece where so much is accomplished with the turn of a faucet or the pressing of a handle, for it was necessary to carry the pitcher of water to the room and lug the slop jar out to the garden or the grape arbor. Yet it had advantages; no mechanical failures requiring expensive visits from the plumber and no exasperating situations when several of the family wish to use the bathroom simultaneously. Today the old fashioned washstand, whether made of pine or mahogany, is eagerly sought by dealers, who sell them to people who put them to strange uses, such as bars or flower stands or radio cabinets.

WATCH BELOW

On shipboard a sailor's off duty time is called his watch below. On the old sailing ships he generally spent this period in the forecastle, the crew's living quarters in the bow of the ship. To reach it he descended a companionway of a few steps; hence his time there was called his "watch below." The sailors slept, washed and mended clothes, spun yarns, sang old songs, thought up new ones, carved articles from wood or whale bone, and one or more of them might always be found with his nose in a book, for mariners have always been great readers. "The watch below" was a term applied to the entire off duty part of the crew, while those at work were "the watch on deck." If the wind freshened and the mate needed more help, there would be a pounding on the forecastle hatchway and the deep water bellow of "all hands," followed by such remarks as "tumble out, look lively now." Then the watch below, with plenty of salt water remarks, would roll out of their bunks or drop whatever they were doing, struggle into their clothes and lay on deck to lend a hand. In the old days the mate was generally ready with the rope's end or a belaying pin or a kick in the stern transom for any seaman who took over long in turning out. When a squall hit a windjammer every hand was needed and no laggard was tolerated.

WATER BAR

A low, gently graded gravel ridge or mound extending across a North Country hill road at a downward angle to carry rain water that collects at one side to the drainage ditch at the other. A culvert would do the job better, but in a thinly settled town where hill roads are numerous and taxpayers are few, a cheaper way was to be found; hence the water bar. The low banking across the road that constitutes a water bar can be made quickly by a man with a shovel and keeps the water from running down the middle of the road and washing away the gravel surface. Of course, a water bar is a bump in the road (a "thank you ma'am"); no problem to a careful driver, but a smart lesson to one who does not know enough to watch ahead. They make nice little jumps for a downhill run on skis.

WATERING CART

In the horse and buggy days when hard paved streets were unknown except downtown, the dust lay inches deep on the roadway in the hot dry summer months. Every horse that trotted by raised a cloud of dust that drifted into open windows, settled down over furniture, rugs and woodwork, leaving

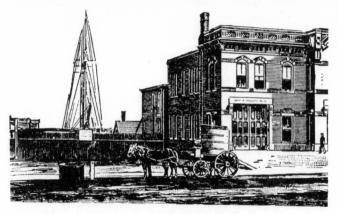

neat housewives exasperated and cranky. Even
downtown enough dust and dried horse manure lay
upon the cobble stones to blow into stores and offices
with every gust. So came the watering cart, a great
advance. A wagon with a round wooden tank and
sprinkler in the rear, drawn by a pair of sleepy
horses, it rumbled up and down the streets, wetting
the dust for a while and giving a dozen barefoot
kids the fun of cavorting about in the spray. In some
towns the watering cart was drawn by a pair of
fire horses and when the whistle blew, the driver
unhitched and headed for the engine house at a gallop to get his steamer or his hose wagon. With paved
streets and mechanical sweepers, the dust nuisance
is eliminated and the watering cart is only a
memory.

WEATHER BREEDER

A clear, cloudless day with extraordinary visibility and little wind. On such days residents along
the coast can see faraway landmarks, such as light-

houses, they could never pick out on an ordinary bright day, this being possibly due to a phenomenon of light refraction on the water. Conditions so perfect are always followed by a particularly mean storm, it is firmly believed, and the true Yankee alters his plans accordingly. Whatever scientific basis for this notion there may be, it is more likely to spring from the feeling of folks in these parts that bad weather is the usual state of affairs and a real good day is an abnormality speedily to be corrected by a stern Mother Nature. The centuries old belief of New Englanders that their weather is a trial visited upon martyrs is being somewhat shaken by the remarks of visitors from other parts of the country who inform us that it could be much worse and proceed to furnish facts and figures.

WEATHER SIGNS

There are dozens of them, enough to fill a book, unreliable half the time, yet interesting to folks who like to talk about the weather, which includes most of us. The accuracy of the signs is, on the average, just about the same as that of the wiseacres who draw good money for discussing the subject on radio and television. However, the old timer who talks about cobwebs on the grass, the signals from his rheumatic joints and the meaning of a red sunset is sensible enough to know this system of his is largely taffy. This fact he expresses in the wisest of his weather maxims; "all signs fail in a dry time."

WEDGE OF GEESE

The high flying v shaped formation of the wild geese on their way to their breeding grounds in the Canadian north in the spring. They talk as they fly, a never ceasing honking sort of converse that leaves landbound man wondering how any living creature can travel at such speed and have left any breath for mere chatter. Perhaps what they say is only sociability, possibly an argument, for from time to time the old gander leading the wedge drops back and another takes the most forward position. Sometimes the formation changes from a wedge to a straight line. The geese fly on into the darkness and sometimes one may hear them, a faint noise in the distance — growing — then directly overhead — talking loudly; at last fading as they wing along into the night, putting the miles behind them. Whoever has lain in bed in the stillness of evening and heard the geese passing over, has known that they are among nature's greatest travelers, never losing their way, pressing on, taking only the barest minimum of rest until journey's end. And the lover of nature who has seen a wedge of geese fly across the face of the full moon will never forget it. In the autumn they are southward bound, headed for marshlands in a climate that has no snow, still talking, pausing only when they hear a honking below them. Then they circle and another family joins their formation, taking its place in the wedge, and on they go. The honking they hear may be from decoys set out by hunters, guns blaze, there are gaps in the wedge, they close up and fly on.

(In states west of us flyways exist, used, no doubt, by wild geese having some unreasonable prejudice against the New England climate.)

WELL SWEEP

To make this primitive device for drawing water, the old settler first chopped down a tree that had a well formed crotch, cut off a piece five feet long and drove it into the ground beside his well. Then he trimmed a stout sapling twenty feet or so long and laid it in the crotch, the short butt end resting on the ground, the other end high above the well, the stick then sloping upward at a 45 degree angle. He fastened a hefty stone, as big as a large punkin, to the butt. To the other end he attached a rope and tied the old oaken bucket to it, so it hung at about ground level. The well sweep was now ready to bring up water. Grasping the rope he hauled downward, the bucket descended into the well, the upper end of the sweep came down, the heavy butt end went up, and the old settler, if he had calculated correctly, found that his bucket was in the water while he still had a little rope left. Then he eased off on the rope, the weighted butt end slowly dropped back to the ground and the long end of the sweep rose, bringing the bucket up to ground level where the man could reach it and hand it to his boy to carry up to the house. The well sweep, an excellent example of the principle of the lever, in this day of electric pumps exists only on the premises of some rare person with a love for things antiquarian.

WENHAM LAKE ICE

The famous ice that Frederic Tudor commenced exporting to the West Indies in sailing ships in 1806. Harvested in Wenham Lake (between Beverly and Wenham) in the dead of winter, it was stored in big ice houses and then drawn for shipment to Cuba, Jamaica, Antigua, St. Kitts and the other islands from time to time during the year. Tudor was a business genius who perfected every detail of his strange trade. Loading his vessels at Salem and Boston, he packed the ice in white pine sawdust so it would keep during the long voyage into tropical waters. He arranged storage facilities in West India ports to keep his cargo from melting immediately upon unloading and he devised crude refrigerators to show his customers how to get the fullest use of his product. Most brilliant stroke of all, he took with him Yankee experts in mixing drinks to demonstrate to the rich planters of those islands the delights of a long, tall, cool one with a sprig of mint on top. Tudor plied his trade, kept his methods to himself and rolled up a very handsome fortune. Others were attracted to the business, many a pond other than Wenham Lake contributed ice to this tropical commerce and a lot of money was made exporting blocks of Yankee zero weather to the hot countries. A great many cargoes were sent to India, which was more difficult because the voyage through warm seas was much longer. A skipper who managed to land half his cargo at Calcutta or Bombay had done well. This traffic continued until late in the 19th century. Rudyard Kipling, who saw everything, has some witty lines on the behavior of a pelican who gobbled up a sliver of ice lying on the wharf at Madras where a Yankee ship was unloading. The bird, with a cold chunk of Wenham Lake in his craw, went through every known contortion until the ice in his gizzard finally melted.

WEST INDIA STORE

A shop dealing largely in products from the Carribbean area; coffee, sugar, molasses, rum, spices and vegetable dyes. Probably one of the first of the specialized type of store, it came into existence in Colonial times as a result of the flourishing trade between New England seaports and Cuba, Haiti, Antigua, Jamaica, St. Vincent and other islands of the West Indies. When the Oriental trade began to grow, after the Revolution, the pepper and tea and cloves and indigo of the East Indies were added to the store keeper's stock in trade. Oranges and lemons from Spanish Florida and the Mediterranean, Canton China, French brandy, and the choice wine of Madeira might be purchased at the West India store by those with a long pocketbook. A rum barrel was always horsed up, liquor was sold by the jug or by the cup, there were plenty of kegs and sugar boxes and full coffee bags to sit on, so it was a convivial place indeed. Some general stores advertised "West India Goods" as a sideline or special department. As this type of merchandise became more common, it was handled by general stores and this specialized shop disappeared in the later part of the 19th Century.

WHIP

A profoundly indecent term used only in Marblehead. Scholars and philologists have engaged in many years of research in Marblehead in an effort to discover the exact meaning of "whip," learning only that it most positively is not a parlor word. A lady not born in Marblehead, upon being told by her son that he had been kept after school for chalking "whip" on the concrete walk, immediately demanded an explanation from the teacher. The teacher was unable to explain why it was wrong, but both she and the boy she had punished were dumbfounded that the mother failed to appreciate the gravity of the offense.

WHISTLE FOR COAL

An expression common in the days of the steam fire engine. On the wide step to the rear of the boiler was limited space in which was carried enough

199

quick-burning cannel coal to keep up steam for the first half hour of operation. If it was a real "working fire," the supply of coal on the engine became exhausted. When he saw his coal getting low, the stoker yanked the whistle cord and a series of long blasts summoned the fire department's coal wagon, which came galloping up with a couple of gunny sacks of fresh fuel. At a big fire, there was frequent whistling as the various steamers, pumping so hard they rocked on their springs, called for the wagon to bring them more coal. And if the fire was at night, citizens lying comfortably in bed in distant dwellings, would hear the varied tones of the whistles and know "the boys" were working on a real tough one.

WIDOW MAKER

The bowsprit or jib boom of a sailing ship. Men making or taking in head sails had to work out on this spar, perched on footropes, one hand for the canvas and the other to hold on. In a real blow the vessel pitched heavily, often putting her bows under and taking green water over her forecastle. When the bowsprit rose again, dripping brine, the mate always counted the men he had sent out there, to see if he still had them all. Too often he was short one, and some woman ashore would be waiting for a man who had gone to Davy Jones. A sailor working on a topsail yard who lost his hold had a chance. If he was clever he might clutch at a stay or brace or halyard as he fell, checking his fall, or possibly hanging on. If he went all the way, he still might fetch up in a coil of rope or a spare sail folded on the deck. Should he strike the hard planking, he was still aboard ship, the captain would fill him up with rum, have two sailors sit on him, and proceed to set his fractured bones according to the directions in the doctor's book carried aboard every vessel. But the man who lost his hold on the bowsprit or jib boom vanished in the boiling seas, perhaps seen briefly by his shipmates as he was swept away, and his woman was a widow.

WIDOW'S WALK

A small platform, fenced in, setting at the highest point of the roof of a house in a New England seaport town. (See Captain's Walk). Here a sailor's wife walked back and forth, looking out to sea for the distant sails of her man's ship. Usually, in the fullness of time, the sail appeared on the horizon and the mariner and his wife were together again, but sometimes a vessel was lost at sea and never heard of again, or made port with her flag at half mast for one of the crew killed in a brush with pirates, or dead with some tropical fever or lost from a topsail yardarm in a storm on the other side of the world. Even when a woman had every reason to believe her man had gone to his last anchorage, the neighbors might see her on the widow's walk staring out to sea, where she had last seen his out-

ward bound ship, never quite giving up her faith that someday he would make home port again. And occasionally her faith was rewarded, for Yankee mariners were a hardy lot, surviving imprisonment in pirate dungeons, shipwrecks and even the dreadful experience of being lost overboard in the night time; at last making their way back to the ones that loved them.

WIGS ON THE GREEN

A first class fight. To appreciate this old New England equivalent of what the Irish call "a Donnybrook," one must recall the day when most men wore powdered wigs and the center of every community was the village green. Easily follows, then, the picture of two old settlers, their wigs lying on the grass near them while they slugged it out, surrounded by a circle of fellow townsmen offering advice and encouragement and perhaps becoming so involved on one side or the other that more fights started, it all ending up with a dozen or two wigs on the green.

WINTER

The annual ninety day sentence New Englanders endure not uncomplainingly or philosophically. In the three Southern New England states it consists of December, January and February, although some wiseacres, for reasons not apparent, propounded the notion that winter is not a matter of weather but of astronomy, commencing at the Solstice about December 21st and ending at the Vernal Equinox about March 21st. These fellows are hard put to it to explain why an ice storm or a six inch snowfall in the first week of December is to be considered autumn weather and the crocus and first robins and green grass of mid-March are to be called winter. More sensible is the view that we have three stages; early winter from Thanksgiving to Christmas, mid-winter from Christmas to Woodchuck Day and late winter from then until St. Patrick's Day. The season can linger. An April blizzard in Massachusetts is no rarity, many a Marathon has been run under leaden clouds spitting snow, the skiing in Tuckerman's Ravine is good in May and there is a cave near the summit of the Smuggler's Notch road in the lee of Mt. Mansfield where snow may sometimes be found on the Fourth of July. Of course the ideal way to spend a winter day is to put one's feet in the oven, light a pipe, and read a good book. The first of those who tried to make the best of this season were the Dartmouth men who pioneered in skiing. Then the Boston & Maine commenced its famous Snow Trains in 1934, the North Country now is dotted with ski tows and hostelries catering to rugged folks and Winter Sports is big business. But most people still welcome a warm turn of weather, even though it spoils the skiing. They envy the birds, who flew South in the autumn, and respect the wisdom of the bear and the woodchuck, who crawled deep into their holes when the frost began to nip, to sleep it out until the sun is again high in the heavens.

WINTER NEVER ROTS IN THE SKY

When there have been some mild weeks and it appears we may be going to get out of it easy, folks up this way say: "Winter never rots in the sky," which is another way of saying that today the lilac buds may look as if they are swelling, but tomorrow morning you may wake up to find a northeast blizzard howling around the corners of the house, a foot of snow on the level and drifting.

WOLF PIT

A trap used by the early settlers to catch wolves, generally a long narrow hole six feet deep with vertical sides made smooth with carefully laid plane faced stone. The roving wolf, who is nocturnal, would fall into this deep pit and being unable to climb up the sheer sides, would be an easy prey to the farmer in the morning. In colonial times wolves were a serious problem, playing havoc with sheep, swine and cattle and attacking people after dark. The old records reveal that the towns offered a bounty of twenty shillings for killing a wolf and in those days that was a very substantial sum of money. An excellent example of a wolf pit is preserved in the Lynn Woods Reservation.

YANKEE NOTIONS

Small articles of an attractive or unusual design, in these times sold in gift shops and at special counters in larger stores. In the days of Yankee sailing ships this expression referred to the items traded with the natives of far away coasts. Stowed in the holds of the Salem and Boston ships were cases of pocket knives, small mirrors, needles, bright colored ribbons, handkerchiefs and beads, razors, chisels and coffee grinders. For such things the Indans of the Northwest Coast would barter sea otter furs, the African chieftans eagerly gave palm oil, ivory and gold dust, and the Sultans of Sumatra supplied pepper berries.

YOUR OX WON'T PLOW

Used by the old settlers in reference to an ox without the strength or will to work to make him a useful animal for the heavy work of pulling a plow, it later came to mean anything not performing the function for which it was intended. An old time judge, after listening to a lawyer make an argument in behalf of his client's case that did not seem at all convincing, disposed of the matter with the simple statement "Your ox won't plow."

ZANZIBAR

 A name so famous in Salem that it has been given to a fancy eating place, a popular candy bar and other commercial products. It is well remembered because upon the Zanzibar trade of the first half of the 19th century were founded some of the town's old fortunes, beautiful mansions were built from the fruits of this commerce and many a family trots out for visitors some curio brought back by an ancestor who was in the crew of a ship that sailed to this Arab port. Situated on a small island near the East African coast half way between the Cape of Good Hope and the Gulf of Aden, it became one of the strongholds of the Arab traders who sailed to all

206

parts of the Indian Ocean in the time of Mohammedan expansion. Here ruled a Sultan who was a very good merchant; peddling elephant ivory, gum copal, cloves, hides and palm oil obtained from the African mainland to Yankee traders, and to the British and French as well. None were smarter than the Salem mariners; they brought to Zanzibar odd lots of lumber and shoes and rum and tobacco and chairs, and always, as the principal cargo item, great quantities of wide cotton sheeting from the newly established Lowell cotton mills. Everyone prospered; the Sultan of Zanzibar and his Arabs, the Lowell spinners, the Lynn shoemakers who thus obtained East African hides, the Yankee factories that used ivory and gum copal and the stores that sold spices. Salem shipmasters retired and came ashore for good and the natives of darkest Africa were able to cover their nakedness with flowing garments of white cotton made in New England.